LIFE
LESSONS LEARNED

LIFE LESSONS LEARNED

Amazing Stories of My Walk Across America for Children

God bless you
Semper Fi
Frank Ryan

FRANCIS X. RYAN, KM, CPA,
COLONEL, USMCR (RET.)

To order additional copies of this book, contact:
Xlibris
1-888-795-4274
www.Xlibris.com
Orders@Xlibris.com
705098

CONTENTS

DEDICATION

I dedicate this book to my dad, who passed away when I was just shy of four years old; to my four children on earth, who put up with me while I learned how to be a father; and to my three children who were miscarried, for whom I pray every day. This book is also dedicated to the most wonderful Sisters of the Good Shepherd, our staff at Good Shepherd, and the magnificent children in our care.

ACKNOWLEDGMENTS

> And the King said to them in reply, "Amen, I say to you, whatever you did for one of these least brothers of mine, you did for me."
>
> —Matthew 25:41

This walk across America would never have been possible without the dedication and tremendous efforts of many people.

First, I want to give special thanks to Diana Ellis and the entire team on the planning committee for this walk. Without their efforts, many of the experiences that I had in these wonderful 148 days would not have been possible.

Diana and her husband, Tae, became my close friends during the walk, and they joined me as I ended the walk on August 9, 2014, in Ocean City, Maryland. Not only were they with me on this last day, but both Diana and Tae were also willing to take calls at all times and all hours to assist while I was walking. For this, I am so grateful.

I thank the Sisters of the Good Shepherd for their prayers and their steadfast devotion to our Savior, our Blessed Mother, and the children entrusted to our care.

Special thanks also go to Dr. Thelma Daley, a very dear friend and spiritual guide for me, who not only serves on the board of directors of Good Shepherd but also put me in touch with the Delta Sigma Theta Sorority and their president, Dr. Paulette Walker, who were so wonderful to me during my journey.

I want to thank our president of Good Shepherd Services, Michele Wyman. Amid changes that could have delayed the walk, Michele stepped up as then acting president, performing with vigor, passion, dedication, and compassion.

Tom Hood, Pam Devine, and all my friends at the Maryland Association of CPAs made this walk especially meaningful. Tom, Pam, et al. went out of their way to put the entire organization behind our efforts.

But the thanks to Tom, Pam, Chris, Emily, Donna, and so many other great friends fail to recognize the history and the depth of the friendship. On three separate occasions during my career and relationship with the MACPA, these wonderful friends were called upon to help me when I was deployed by the United States Marine Corps Reserve. Not once did they complain about the inconvenience that I had placed on them when I called them at the last minute as I left the country. To say that they did not complain underscores the tremendous support they gave me while away. For that, I am extremely grateful.

It is also important that I acknowledge the great support and friendship that I received from my friends at Western CPE as well as all the state societies of CPAs and the AICPA.

During my walk, I was honored to spend three days walking with a dear friend, Doug Sethness. Doug met me on the road just outside of Dalhart, Texas. He accompanied me through all of Texas and most of Oklahoma.

Doug and I served together at the US Special Operations Command Central during Operation Enduring Freedom in Afghanistan. I saw him act under intense pressure with complete integrity, dignity, and professionalism. Doug, you are a hero to me, my friend.

During my walk, I met some incredibly wonderful people. I am grateful as they made this walk truly memorable.

This walk would never have been completed if it had not been for my dear friend Greg Conderacci. Every day without fail, Greg sent me a note, e-mail, or words of encouragement. Greg, thank you.

To our spiritual director, Father William Kuchinsky, I wanted to extend my heartfelt thanks and prayers for your friendship, prayers, and guidance throughout these past few years. God bless you.

And finally, from the bottom of my heart, I want to thank my family, particularly Sherrie and my children, for allowing me to be away once more. During this walk, Sherrie's father, John Costa, passed away. May he rest in peace.

PURPOSE OF THE WALK

In 2008, our nation faced a serious financial crisis. During that crisis, funding for mental health became disrupted and services were underfunded.

While this crisis brought the issue that led to the walk to the surface, the thought process behind the walk and the need to raise awareness of the needs of children with emotional and behavioral problems occurred much earlier.

In the mid to late 1980s, Good Shepherd and the sisters saw a major change in focus by regulators in dealing with childhood behavioral issues. Funding for routine early-intervention therapies almost evaporated. At that time, only children with severe behavioral issues were being treated, but only after the problem had reached a crisis stage.

As I examined what regulatory bodies were saying and then examining what we were seeing in the community, I noticed a disconnect between reality and public policy.

We were seeing significantly more severe cases, and caseworkers noticed significant behavioral issues in schools.

When we questioned the efficacy of certain programs along with state and federal policies, we were quoted studies the basis of which did not seem to reflect the reality of what our staff were seeing.

As certified public accountants (CPA), we are taught to be professionally skeptical. Professional skepticism means for us to question everything that affects our mission. CPAs are also required to not subordinate our judgment, meaning we are not to take the easy way out.

When I questioned the studies being used to base public policy on, I was not convinced of the soundness of the study. If the study was not sound, public policy would be ineffective, children would be hurt, and the problems would get worse.

The facts were not supporting what we were seeing in policy. This is a recipe for disaster to society and the children needing help.

At the same time I was noticing this public policy concerns, I had independently been thinking about walking across America for personal reasons.

My personal reasons were that I wanted a chance to reflect on life. I wanted my walk to be a walk of atonement and gratitude.

From the perspective of the walk of gratitude first, I always told people that I came from a very poor family. My dad died when I was three years old, and my mom was left with five children to support with little visible means of support. My younger sister was six months old when my dad died, and my mom was just thirty-six years old.

Imagine yourself as a thirty-six-year-old with five children from age six months to twelve years old and no money. In 1955, insurance was not readily available, and my dad was probably uninsurable because he had lung cancer.

My mom, with the help of my grandmother and my aunt Marie, wonderful folks in our community in the Catholic Church in Baltimore, was able to pull it together. But she struggled. I believe her financial struggles became the basis of my lifetime avocation of helping people avoid bankruptcy.

I recall seeing Mom crying late one night because she was having trouble making ends meet. She saw me. She explained that it was going to be okay and tried to hide her fear. I knew better.

I often think that I started my turnaround consulting practice that day.

Years later, after seeing what many of the children at Good Shepherd have gone through, I realized that I was not poor at all. In fact, I realized that I came from an extremely wealthy family who just happened to not have any money. I never once doubted that my mom and my brothers and sisters and family loved me.

The children of Good Shepherd and the sisters have taught me to be grateful for the wonderful gifts that I have been granted caretaker of.

In addition to the walk of gratitude, the walk across America was for a walk of atonement.

The walk of atonement was intended to be a time to reflect and ask those people that I have hurt in my life to forgive me, those people in my life whom I have disappointed to pray for me, and those people in my life that I have helped, that they would help another.

It is amazing to me how the death of a parent can have such a profound impact on one's life.

I often think and I saw in my own family, and in others' families and in some of the families of the children at Good Shepherd, that mistakes that we make are rooted in our own responsibility and are affected deeply by what we experienced as children.

I have often seen books that discuss a person's great achievements. The publications reinforce the great things that someone has done, but frequently, the books gloss over the trials and tribulations that have affected that person's life. Many times, this glossing over is because most people keep those trials and tribulations very close to their hearts so many people may not know the trials.

So my walk of atonement was a hope that I would reverse that trend and deal head-on with the mistakes that I have made in my life, which, in my faith, I call sins, so that others can benefit from learning about failing, forgiveness, and atonement.

My brother Bob and I often talked about our perception of our dad and mom. We were at different ages when Dad died. Dad was extremely ill, and Mom and Dad were both in their midthirties.

For those of you that read this book that are in your fifties and sixties, you will look back at amusement about your thirties, when you recognize and admit that life was pretty good at that age.

Bob and I admitted that most of the mistakes and sins that we have done that had horrible consequences occurred later in life. I wondered what advice I would have listened to, to avoid these errors.

Life lessons are learned the hard way. I was convinced there had to be a better way to learn than the hard way.

I realized later in life that I learned much more from my mistakes than I had from my successes. It seemed logical to me that one of the greatest gifts I could give to my children would be to tell them about my struggles and failings rather than about my successes.

The walk became that opportunity to write about, pray about, and seek forgiveness. Atonement goes well beyond being forgiven. As a Catholic, I know that my Savior forgives my sins, but that does not alleviate my responsibility to atone for what I have done or what I have failed to do.

If you are not of faith, this may not make much sense to you, but I would encourage you to reflect on those people you have hurt, those that you have disappointed, and those that you have helped.

Should you find that task to be difficult, I would encourage you to think about those people who have hurt you, those people who disappointed you, and those people that have helped you. When you do this, you may find that all you have to do is transition from looking at yourself to looking at how others are affected by you. It is an eye-opening experience. It is a heartwarming experience. It is the final stage of forgiveness, to be able to atone for what you have done.

When atonement is sought, behaviors change. The cycle of forgiveness is then complete, and true family healing can occur.

With this walk of atonement and gratitude, Diana Ellis and I discussed using it as well as an opportunity to talk about the needs of children with emotional, behavioral, and developmental disabilities.

That is how the walk of atonement and gratitude became a walk across America for children. I was hoping that during my walk, the Holy Spirit would guide me and give me the wisdom that I would need to develop a program to help children in need independent of financing.

I became convinced that only by looking at the problem of children's needs from a compassionate perspective could we hope to have a meaningful faith-based solution to the problem.

When a problem such as emotional, behavioral, and developmental disabilities is dealt with as a cost, the person and their family are lost in the endeavor.

By the same token, by not being concerned with treating children effectively and compassionately, we may fail to solve the problem and inadvertently perpetuate a treatment methodology that may or may not be effective.

So in my walk, I was praying that the Holy Spirit would guide me in developing a logical yet compassionate process so that we can continuously question our methods as we try to help children and their families.

In other words, solve the problem!

Little did I know that the lessons I had hoped to learn were overwhelmed by the life's lessons learned while walking across America.

WALK PLANNING

The planning for the walk across America was a lengthy process.

The planning included my mental and physical preparedness and the planning done by the staff that volunteered to assist in mapping the route and in developing the logistics along the way.

In terms of the mental and physical preparedness, you should consider that a walk of this nature is more of a mental effort than a physical one.

People that I have talked with have asked when I began training to walk across America. Invariably, I would explain that my training began as a youngster, was further developed when I was in the Marine Corps, and then expanded to include my day-to-day life. In reality, the specific physical training began in earnest in September 2012 and was almost nonstop from January 1, 2013, until I left for the walk on March 15, 2014.

The preparations were pretty significant since much of what I learned in my early life and in the Marine Corps helped with the walk, but in some cases, they hindered it.

By the end of the walk, I realized that many things I learned were more about leadership and questioning assumptions than about walking. As a result, the focus of the book became those life's lessons that I learned on this amazing adventure.

Life Lessons Learned **Preparedness is as much a mental state as a physical condition.**

After the walk, I realized that much of the training in my entire life was done in a sterile environment. Things that I had learned in training turned out to have a negative impact on me while walking. Training did not replicate real life. I have seen such a disconnect in so many areas of my life.

Life Lessons Learned: **Working hard with a plan yields positive results; without a plan, it yields disaster.**

In the military and in other aspects of my business life, I did things in short spurts. There were periods of extremely intense effort followed by periods of recuperation. When walking across America, one quickly realizes that the walk is a much more prolonged effort in which stamina is significantly more important than strength. It is truly the difference between running a hundred-meter dash versus running a marathon.

Life Lessons Learned: **Stamina trumps brute force all the time—the tortoise versus the hare!**

All my training reinforced short-term training goals, but my training did not anticipate the long-term aspects of the walk.

I found out very quickly, by March 20, 2014, or six days into the walk, that my training was inadequate for what I was doing. It was adequate from the physical aspect, but it was inadequate from the aspect of the long-term nature of a hundred-day-plus walk.

None of my prior experiences or training prepared me for what I was about to undertake. That in and of itself was a learning experience in that short-term quick-fix solutions may work very well in the short run but are disastrous in the long run.

Life Lessons Learned: **Potential solutions must emulate real-life situations to be effective.**

From September 2 to September 5, 2013, I walked thirty-two miles per day to get ready for the thirty-two miles per day that I planned on doing during my walk across America. I completed the four days of training extremely well and none the worse for wear. I actually thought that I could extrapolate four days into one hundred and all would be well.

Was I ever wrong!

I have included some of the lessons learned from that four-day trial as an appendix. There were tons of other lessons I should have learned, however, that I would learn shortly after I started walking in March 2014.

The four days of training was the way we would have done it in my early life, in the military, and in short spurts of activity while I was in business. The physical and mental demands of thirty-two miles per day for one hundred days were something I never anticipated.

Fortunately, I had mentally prepared myself for this walk my entire life in the sense that I was prepared to be uncomfortable, to be exhausted, and to be in pain.

Diana Ellis assembled a fantastic team of volunteers to assist in the planning effort. The volunteers included Diana Ellis, director of development of Good Shepherd; fellow board member Will Butterazzi; our former president, Dr. Derrick Boone; Bobby Baird, our CFO at that time; Brian Hadleman, volunteer; Janna Krizman; and Nicole Brown. Michele Wyman, our current president, and Regina Malloy were also extremely helpful on the committee once the walk started.

The work by the volunteers included route planning, making contacts in different dioceses and archdioceses that I would walk through, as well as seeking the assistance of the Knights of Columbus to help me along the way. Additionally, Dr. Thelma Daley of our board of directors was extraordinarily helpful in having the Delta Sigma Theta (the Deltas) sorority help us.

This walk would not have been possible without the extraordinary efforts of the planning committee and the Deltas. I will be forever grateful for their kindness and generosity of their time, compassion, and assistance.

The walk committee culminated its efforts with the training walk that we all did from Fort McHenry in downtown Baltimore, to the Archdiocese of Baltimore Cathedral, to my boyhood home on Glenhunt Road, all the way to Good Shepherd Services. It was an unbelievable time to reflect on the kindness and efforts of so many great people.

We had a number of decisions to make at the very beginning that brought into focus the planning and execution of this walk across America.

The actual route selection was fairly significant in and of itself. I personally had a number of constraints that had a major impact on the route selection. The biggest constraint was that I was still working full-time, so I had to be very careful about how much time I was away from work, since I had people that were depending on me to generate business leads and income for them.

The beginning part of the year seemed to me to be the best time to walk. Route selection was very definitely affected by my work schedule. Specifically, I chose to start around March 15 because of weather, it was a slower time of year in my business, and most of my corporate taxes would be done by then.

Because I was starting on March 15 and because of my concern about weather, we selected a southern route starting in San Diego. San Diego afforded the greatest opportunity to have fairly decent weather in the beginning.

I had considered leaving from San Francisco and walking through some of the trails there but decided against that since many of the trails would not open until May 15.

We knew from the onset that using San Diego as the starting point would be a challenge, because I would be leaving Pennsylvania toward the end of winter, when temperatures were about twenty-five degrees to thirty-five degrees, and begin walking from San Diego with temperatures easily in the mideighties.

I had trained in the Marine Corps to deal with those temperature changes, but I did not truly appreciate the fact that I was no longer twenty-five years old. I was somewhat surprised that this one assumption had such a big impact on me.

From San Diego, our goal included stopping at certain critical locations along the way, which helped define the route. Specifically, we wanted to stop and visit the Sisters of the Good Shepherd in Saint Louis. This one stop essentially because the route to go from a southern route to a midwestern route to a northern route by the end of the trip.

Originally, our planning was to have me do thirty-two miles per day for eleven days straight with one day off and try to get done by July 1. The plan was so tight because of the need to get back to work since I had decided upfront that I was going to cover all the costs of this walk personally so that any money that we did raise would go to the children.

Some of the reasons for choosing July 1 included work consideration as well as a desire to walk into the Maryland Association CPA beach retreat in Ocean City as a grand finale. The significance of the thirty-two miles per day was that I was averaging four miles per hour in training and presumed that I could keep that pace and walk eight hours per day to give me enough time to recuperate. This assumption was a very serious flaw in my planning process.

Life Lessons Learned: **Optimism is great; realism is better.**

We did have a contingency plan in case I was injured during the walk. I kept my work schedule light after July 1 into August 31 in case injuries kept me from finishing by July 1. It was also one of the reasons I walked from the West Coast to the East Coast. The thought was that if I was not able to finish by July 1, I would finish the walk closer to home on weekends.

Walking from the West Coast, we knew, was going to present a challenge due to weather changes from the East Coast to the West Coast at that time of year, as well as the fact that all my support contacts were on the East Coast.

One of our board members, Will Butterazzi, had a suggestion that we contact the various dioceses and archdioceses along the route as well as use the Knights of Columbus for assistance. Will did a tremendous job of organizing that. Some of the letters of support that we received are included as appendices. Will thought that it would be a good idea, and I agreed to have a letter of introduction from the archbishop of Baltimore, Archbishop Lori, and Sister Mary Catherine of the Sisters of the Good Shepherd. Both of those ideas were extremely useful when I was walking. I thought you would enjoy seeing the letters, so I have included them as an appendix.

The route map

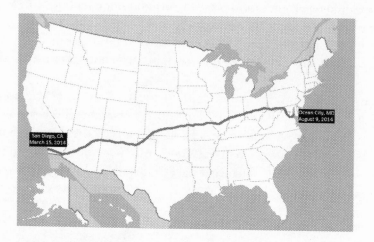

While planning the logistics, I trained by walking and trying out my gear. During the most latter part of training, I completed over 1,500 miles.

In training, I tried to find locations where I would go up and down hills that would test my stamina, types of food that I would need, and the adequacy of the equipment. I have included as an appendix the list of the equipment that I thought I would need.

In testing out the gear, I wanted to find out what impact different types of shoes and backpacks would have on the walk. The value of packing light became important during this part of the training evolution. However, I would never truly appreciate the value of packing light until I started the walk on March 15.

Life Lessons Learned: **Pack light; baggage is heavy! This is true for emotional baggage as well as physical baggage.**

There is the idea of packing light, and there is the reality of packing light.

During training, the impact of carrying too much equipment was not readily apparent. One lesson I learned is that what you experience in the short run does not necessarily translate into the experiences that you need for the long run where stamina and energy can be exhausted by carrying too much equipment.

During a farewell party at Good Shepherd, a very dear friend of mine, Greg Conderacci, gave me a piece of advice about packing and carrying only what I really need. That admonition probably saved my life.

***Life Lessons Learned*: Real friends tell you what you need to hear, not what you want to hear.**

The role of trust comes to play as well. I trusted Greg implicitly, and that trust was well-founded. Learning that simple lesson of being able to trust someone was critical during the walk, when fatigue clouded my judgment. I would not appreciate the significance of trust until I was midway through the walk.

The same issue of trust was reinforced as I started to think about our children at Good Shepherd. They must be able to trust us. I was reminded that trust is a gift that others give us.

The value of trust was not as apparent during my training as it was during the walk. The value of trust became clearly understood within days of my departure from San Diego.

***Life Lessons Learned*: Trust is the blood of life—hard to earn, easy to lose.**

I recognized the value of trust when I remembered that my walk was a walk of atonement. I encourage you to think about those people in your life that may have lost the ability to trust you. I encourage you to try to earn that trust back one step at a time. I learned during my training and during this walk that trust is built up over a lifetime but destroyed in a second.

During my training walks, I always dedicated each day's walk to those that I was praying for.

My intent with the daily petitions was to recognize the faith-based nature of the walk and to let people know that I was beginning the walk of atonement and gratitude even during the training phase. I found that by praying the rosary daily and dedicating the prayer to our Savior, the Holy Trinity, and the Blessed Mother, I would become closer to remembering that this walk must be about others.

The goal in the walk was to develop a methodology and framework to help children in need. It was absolutely critical to me that this not be about me doing a walk but about why I was doing the walk. Doing something for the wrong reason minimizes the atonement reasons for the walk in my mind. Doing the walk for personal gain will be like the person who is proud of their humility. It was important to me that this walk and this book be about all those other people whom I have hurt and am asking forgiveness from, those I have disappointed and am asking for prayers, and those that I have helped and am asking to help others.

Each day's training walk gave me an opportunity to reflect and connect with those people that I was praying for and for their families. The daily blogs spurred the dialogue about what was so important in helping our children.

This dialogue below on January 1, 2013, was with the mother of one of our Malades with whom I went to Lourdes. Terri and Faith and her family became very close friends. I was impressed with their spirituality and their love for our Savior and our Blessed Mother.

January 1, 2013

Terri,

May I ask you a huge favor?

I am training for a Walk across America and I dedicate prayers and a rosary each day to someone important in my life.

Might I ask you to tell Faith that I am going to say a rosary tomorrow (January 2nd) for her. The Glorious Mysteries are on my schedule and I will make sure that I remember her throughout my trip.

You and your family made such a huge impact on me. God bless you and tell Faith she is my heroine!

Semper fi,

Frank

In this simple exchange, I wanted Faith to know that while distance may have kept our families apart, she and our families would be forever connected spiritually.

The day of prayer was an important one for me because I had not been able to see Faith and her family since my return from the pilgrimage due to work commitments and training for the walk.

Being overcommitted became a recurring theme in my walk of atonement.

Life Lessons Learned: **Overcommitting serves no one. Learn to say no and when to say yes.**

Prioritize what is important and do not attempt to be everything to everyone, or you will find out that you are nothing to anyone. Do not let others waste your time.

Life Lessons Learned: **Focus on what is important, because everything else is a distraction.**

Embracing the unexpected and welcoming the unexpected became one of the greatest mental challenges during the walk. When I was walking during training and when I was walking across America, I tried to reflect on the core values of the Sisters of the Good Shepherd.

Those core values are mercy, individual worth, reconciliation, and zeal.

Life Lessons Learned: **Embrace the unexpected.**

Life Lessons Learned: **Mercy, individual worth, reconciliation, and zeal.**

January 8, 2013

Ken and Ann,

I am training for a walk across America for children.

I dedicated each day a rosary for the special intentions of the day.

This Thursday, I am dedicating the walk and the rosary of the Luminous Mystery to Andy Ward, Andy Ward Jr and Andy's wife. I would like to you both and your brother for his time with Christ in Heaven to my walk for the day if that is ok with you? If it is, can you send me his full name?

You both have touched me deeply with your caring and love for your brother. I wish I had known him.

Semper fi,

Frank

In this simple exchange is something that became very important to me during the walk. Ken and Ann Urish are two very dear friends of mine. Ken and Ann were absolutely devoted to Ann's brother, who was a special-needs young man. I wanted to pray for Ken, Ann, and other friends with children or relatives with disabilities and thank them for their wonderful zeal and mercy to Christ's special children.

I often looked back in my own life and questioned the times when I felt overwhelmed and maybe became short with people. I then looked at people who had significant challenges in their lives and tried to help them with the dignity and grace they deserved.

These prayers for my friends during my training walk were intended to remind me of how I should be versus how I sometimes am. It was the essence of my walk of gratitude that I would never take for granted the wonderful gifts or obstacles in front of me so that I would accept everything with dignity, zeal, mercy, reconciliation, and persistence.

Hi Frank,

Happy New Year! I am glad to hear from you. It is exciting to hear about your walk across America. We would be honored and feel blessed to be included in your dedication. Here are our names:

Kara

Spouse: Paul

Son: Jack"

I've also included a photo I took with my phone this past Saturday of Jack. It was his first day at a Saturday-only preschool program. We were so proud of him and we continue to be amazed at how hard this little guy works each day.

Thank you for putting me back in touch with the Wards. Dorothy is a wonderful mentor to myself.

Take care as you train for your walk!

Semper Fi,

Kara

When I was in Minnesota in 2013, I met Kara, and I had mentioned the walk for children with emotional, behavioral, and developmental disabilities. Kara told me about her son Jack and the challenges he was facing. With tears in her eyes, you could see the love and devotion she had for her son and her husband. I told Kara that Jack and her entire family would be in my prayers during my walk.

Whenever I started to feel overwhelmed during the walk or in training, I remembered Jack, Ann's brother, Andy Jr., and all our children past, present, and yet to come at Good Shepherd. I vowed not to let them down.

In the early part of 2014, the magnitude of the walk and the 2,806 miles became apparent to me when, at the same time, the weather on the East Coast deteriorated significantly.

I realized that my training was going to be adversely affected in the January to March 14, 2014, time frame because of all the snow we were having on the East Coast. I was concerned that my training in snow and ice might trigger an injury prior to my kickoff date.

I made the decision to save energy and reduce the risk of injury by doing maintenance walks of eight or nine miles four days a week prior to leaving for California.

The mental work that needed to be done prior to leaving was astonishing, so I was not even sure if I would have had more time to train anyway. I travelled to Bozeman, Montana, for five days in February to record courses for continuing professional education, and while I was there, it was thirty degrees below zero! That certainly was going to be a significant difference in the temperature that I was going to be feeling in less than fifteen days. In reality, the temperature swing was 140 degrees in fifteen days. Wow! What an experience! Embrace the unexpected.

To have sufficient income while I was away, I spent a week in Dallas, lecturing to an industry conference for certified public accountants. It was a chance to reflect less than two weeks before the start of the walk.

February 27, 2014

Please join Frank for the Walk Across America Kick-Off on Thursday, March 6, 2014 from 11am–1pm at Good Shepherd. The Bistro Lunch Box Food Truck which will be parked near the front steps of Good Shepherd with delicious food for sale, and 10% of the proceeds will go to Good Shepherd.

I was honored that my friends at Good Shepherd, to include our staff and board and my dear friends at the Maryland Association of CPAs, along with one of my closest friends, Greg Conderacci, were able to join with me on our kickoff event.

I was so thankful that Jamie Costello of ABC news in Baltimore, who has since become a close friend, was able to join us for an interview before the kickoff.

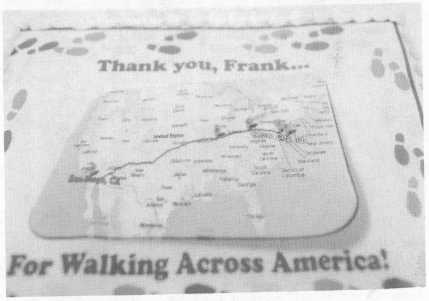

The kickoff event brought home how close it was to my leaving and how much I still had to do.

At the kickoff event, I received a number of prayer petitions. I was delighted to add those prayer petitions to my entire list of those that I would pray for each day while I was walking.

March 4, 2014

Getting excited about the journey! Please send me your prayer petitions.

I would be honored to carry your concerns and worries throughout my journey.

Does anyone know how many miles I should expect to get on the pair of shoes before I have to have them retreaded? :-)

That question that I asked about how long I should expect to get out of a pair of shoes was an interesting one. I answered it somewhat in jest but also somewhat seriously when I said that I brought two pairs of shoes, and I thought that that would be enough. How wrong I would be.

In the 1,500 miles of training that I had done, I did not go through one pair of shoes, or so I thought. Shortly after I started the walk on March 15, 2014, I realized that I did not even know when a pair of shoes was already worn out. That was another major learning experience for me as I realized by the end of the journey that I had eight pairs of shoes and had worn out four of them before I was done walking across America. What a wakeup call.

Life Lessons Learned: Nothing, no matter how seemingly trivial, is trivial. Shoes almost ended my journey. Every part of the team is critical.

March 6, 2014

The kickoff luncheon and party was a time to reflect with friends and to remember why we were doing this walk.

I think one of the most heartfelt moments came from the kind words of my dear friend Greg Conderacci when he told me that he had a vested interest in seeing me make it home safely. His friendship stayed with me every single day of the walk.

When I received prayer petitions from the staff at Good Shepherd asking me to pray for some of our runaways, I realized the selfless sacrifice of our staff, who are concerned first and foremost for our children. God bless them, and thank you for sharing your fears and your concerns with me.

March 7, 2014

I had an opportunity to go on WLBR radio, 1270, today with my dear friend Laura LeBeau, who was kind enough to invite me to talk about the walk across America, the Sisters of the Good Shepherd, and most importantly, our children!

March 13, 2014

> *Tomorrow's the day! I leave for San Diego at 3PM and start walking back home on the 15th! Please send your prayer requests. Spent much time today with my friends at the MACPA and saying farewell. WLBR and my dear friend Laura LeBeau gave a great sendoff as did her fellow journalist—Gordon Weise.*

As I was completing the last-minute details for getting ready to walk, I finally received the cart that I was going to be using for the first half of my walk. Diana Ellis and Bobby Baird suggested that I take a cart with me to carry my equipment since I was going to be carrying so much gear for the trip.

During the kickoff event in the days preceding my leaving, Greg Conderacci reminded me to pack light. Truer words were never said.

After completing the walk, I realized how many things I would do differently.

I am convinced that we may be victims of our own experiences. Obviously, the training I had in the United States Marine Corps was very helpful, but it was a different type of training and real-life experience than what I was about to undertake.

Life Lessons Learned: **Do not let life's experiences limit how you think and how you respond.**

I could not help but wonder if my training from September 2012 until I left was somewhat jaundiced by what I thought I was about to be doing rather than what I actually encountered.

I realized that perhaps every endeavor results in the same type of learning experience in which reality must improve both theory and our approach to solving problems.

When I was walking, I was often asked by people who visited the blog what training I recommended, what gear was needed, and how we selected the route.

One of the first lessons learned was that you should practice with all your equipment for months before going on a journey of this nature. There were many things that I found out about my equipment, particularly the cart, that would have been very useful to learn before I left. For example, I was going to be in the mountains for much of the early part of the journey, so having a cart with a brake on it would have been smart. The results of that decision will be shown by the fifth day of the walk.

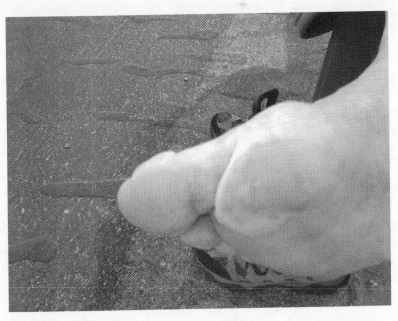

Additionally, it was a mistake to go from negative thirty degrees in Bozeman, Montana, in February, to twenty-five to thirty degrees in Pennsylvania in mid-March, to San Diego, California, on March 14 at eighty degrees, and start walking on March 15 at 8:00 AM with temperatures reaching the high eighties by the end of the day. While we got through it, it was not well thought out and could have caused problems. This was one lesson about acclimatization that I was well aware of and should not have forgotten.

Becoming acclimatized also reminded me that we need to give our children and our staff time to become acclimatized to any changes or structural changes that we may be considering in our desire to help our children better, or the effects of the change can be disruptive.

Life Lessons Learned: **A great leader calmly introduces changes that are planned, or chaos ensues.**

While I had trained most of my life to expect the unexpected, the ability to adapt to change is important, or the results can be catastrophic.

I would also recommend to anyone who attempts any new challenge, research as much as you possibly can and learn from others who have done similar things. Each person's experiences will be different, but the conceptual issues and learning will usually be the same.

Life Lessons Learned: **Research and challenging assumptions and widely held beliefs are critical to the success of any plan.**

If I had to do it over again, I would also recommend that planning include a dry run or simulation of what you are planning so that you have a better understanding of the logistics.

My not doing a dry run created some issues that could have ended the walk. First, I brought more equipment than I needed for the first thirty days. The extra weight meant that I had to transport it, which expended energy for no benefit. The realization of how much wasted effort takes place in so many programs was the first thing that came to mind.

Second, by not being familiar with the route, the elevation changes, which are not clear on a two-dimensional map, become all too real the second you begin the walk.

Third, understanding where I can resupply each day would have been very useful.

One of the goals of the walk was to rely on faith to provide for me. I had absolute faith that I would be provided for during the walk, but I really did not anticipate how much time the logistics would take in order to be able to walk thirty-two miles a day, let alone twenty-five miles per day.

The implications of the logistics of the walk were much more significant than I expected.

I found that in order to walk twenty-five miles per day, it took me the better part of fourteen hours to walk and plan the logistics.

During my training, I carried a fairly heavy backpack of between twenty-five and fifty pounds, and I was able to average four miles per hour. Once I started walking on March 15, however, I never got over three miles per hour. I had been cautioned that maintaining a four-mile-per-hour pace was not sustainable, but it had been so easy in training. The speed admonition was one that I should have listened to more carefully.

By the opposite token, I also found that you had to be careful about the advice that you took. Many cases occurred in which I was cautioned about not doing something, but in order to accomplish the walk, I had to do it. I did it with some fear and trepidation, only to find out that my advisors' perspective was based upon their experiences, which had nothing to do with my experiences or reality.

Life Lessons Learned: **Pick your advisors carefully, but it is ultimately your judgment and your decision.**

I cannot emphasize enough that you have to have the judgment to know when to listen and the judgment and wisdom to know when not to. I also found that you must have your trusted advisors, those people with positive energy, whom you can rely on to give you unfiltered advice.

If you are a negative person or surround yourself with people who sap your energy, you will never complete a walk or any major endeavor. You have to be positive that you are resourceful enough and prayerful enough to find solutions to any and every problem that you face.

Great leaders understand the value of a positive attitude, but that becomes an even greater source of strength when you are continuously tested by the unexpected. Come to embrace the unexpected, and you will have all the preparation you will ever need for a walk across America or any other challenge that you may undertake.

Life Lessons Learned: **Positive attitudes win. Negative attitudes are energy thieves.**

Finally, train as you expect to operate. Training in pain helps you deal with pain. When training, I would try to push myself close to heat exhaustion to learn how to deal with it and to recognize the symptoms when they appeared. I did the same thing with hypothermia and found both to be extremely helpful during the walk.

March 14, 2014

> *Frank is off to San Diego!* — *with Frank Ryan and Diana Ellis.*
>
> *Michele, Diana, and the Sisters will be meeting me here at the airport shortly.*
>
> *No turning back now! :-) just think only 14,277,184 more steps to go when I'm done. :)*
>
> *As I head out the door—no keys, no watch, no computer— ok, I just did not realize that my "support" system has abandoned me! :) Thanks to my son, Matt for staying with us while I am away.*

*Leaving for the airport! Thanks to all who have offered
prayers and support. Let us all give thanks to our Savior,
our Children entrusted to our care and to the Sisters of the
Good Shepherd.*

I rented a car in Hershey, Pennsylvania, in order to go to the airport to
fly to San Diego. I flew out of Baltimore on Southwest Airlines because
it was more convenient, and quite candidly, I like Southwest Airlines.

The staff at Southwest Airlines was unbelievably helpful in having me
check my equipment.

At the airport, I met Michele, Diana, and the Sisters of the Good
Shepherd, who were so kind as to bring me a rosary to use on my
journeys. What a wonderful sendoff and great reminder about why we
were doing this.

I would not be honest with you if I did not let you know that I was
getting nervous about what was about to happen. The moment of
truth had arrived. I had always said that one of my biggest fears was
not being able to complete this walk for whatever reason and thereby
disappoint our children. I felt, in many cases, many of our children have
been disappointed by adults, and that thought was running through
my mind.

I needed our children to know that we would be there for them no
matter what. Many of our children are very fortunate to have parents
who are very supportive and care for them, and we have some parents
who need help in understanding how they can best help their children.

*Just arrived in San Diego. Everyone has been so kind. Met
a classmate from my MBA program at the University of
Maryland. He doesn't look as old as I do. :(*

With all these wonderful experiences, I would do it again as I did on
March 14, 2014.

THE WALK!

Go Frank Ryan! I will be thinking about, praying, and social media supporting your journey! Can't wait to see you in Ocean City! Stay hydrated!

—Comment from Jody Padar, March 15, 2014

The first comment that I received was from my dear friend and fellow instructor Jody Padar.

As I was gathering my gear to begin the walk from the beaches in San Diego, I thought about these kind words. Do not ever forget the value of kindness and the impact that it can have on another person's life. I would hope that if you do appreciate the value of kind words, you would also appreciate the impact of negative words and how hurtful they can be, particularly to children.

Life Lessons Learned: **Be kind.**

Alberto was kind enough to help me from the airport, to his home, to dinner around San Diego, and finally to the kickoff point on March 15 on the beaches in San Diego. So many of my friends came to join me that day, particularly John and Cynthia Lovewell, Joyce and the Deltas, and some well-wishers who met me on the airplane coming from Baltimore to San Diego and wanted to wish me well. What a great feeling that was.

I am in shorts, and Alberto is dressed in winter clothing because he thinks it is cold and I think it is hot. Life is all about perspective.

I was wearing shorts, and that lasted for about four days. The temperature was in the mideighties, so it sounded like a reasonable thing to do, but I was as pale as pale can be! Within six hours, I had the beginnings of sun poisoning on my legs, and I thought it was not going to end well if I did not get covered up. By the fifth day, I was wearing long pants and did not have any problems after that.

By the end of the first day, I had people stopping me on the road and asking if I was okay when they saw the splotches on my legs. *Splotches* seemed like such a great word when you saw what they looked like, because there was nothing pretty about it. As my brother Bob would say, "Those are the legs that only a mother could love."

When I was walking, I noticed sights throughout that reminded me of my faith. In one particular picture, I saw three flowers, which reminded me of the Holy Trinity. The tranquility of walking was already taking hold.

I saw scenery that reminded me of the beauty of our children. It reminded me of what the sisters always said, that we save one child at a time.

When I passed through the San Diego City limit after walking about five hours, the magnitude of what I was about to do sank in. I passed a number of Marine Corps installations that brought back some very fond memories of my days in the Marine Corps but also reminded me that after five hours, I was still at the starting point.

After completing about twenty-six miles, my day was done, and I was waiting to get picked up and driven to the hotel. The plan was to walk a prescribed distance and then coordinate with folks who would volunteer to pick me up and take me to a hotel or to their homes.

I had an interesting thing happen as I was sitting in a parking area, waiting for a ride to the hotel. A person by the name of Jan Jensen stopped with her friend and asked me if I needed any help. I explained to her what I was doing. She was very supportive and offered to help us the next day. Not only did Jan help that next day, but she also coordinated with people to help me for the next five days after that.

That evening, Joyce and Monique of the Deltas picked me up and took me to the hotel, which the Deltas were so gracious to sponsor. I would be less than honest with you if I did not tell you how exhausted I was, so their help was wonderful.

The excitement and adrenaline of starting the walk were exhilarating, but reality set in as well. The temperature difference from the East Coast to the West Coast in March 2014 was far more significant than I expected, and I was not yet acclimated.

I did not get the number of miles in that I expected to for a whole variety of reasons, most of which was because I was carrying significantly more weight than I needed. Joyce and Monique were very helpful in assisting me in solving part of that problem, but it was not until about the tenth day that that the weight problem of excess equipment had been resolved completely.

Not getting the miles in for the plan was not as upsetting to me as I thought it might be, because there were so many things going on. Little did I know that my plan of thirty-two miles per day was just not achievable since I was not making the speed that I hoped for. Once the realization set in that I was not going make the speed that I had hoped for, I knew for certain that I was not going to complete the journey by July 1, which was a devastating realization.

Life Lessons Learned: **The real character of a person comes out when failure is apparent.**

I was also taken aback by the amount of calories that I was consuming. Despite eating huge quantities of food, I was still burning energy.

Only then did I remember the advice I received from Greg and Michele. They both warned me to eat from the moment I started in the morning and continue through the day. They suggested that, for lack of a better term, I should "graze." This would turn out to be extraordinarily sound advice, because the moment you find yourself out of energy, it is too late. You need to be consuming food to give you the energy you need all the time.

Life Lessons Learned: **By the time you realize you have a problem, it is already too late.**

Joyce and Monique were very helpful at asking me what supplies I needed for the next day, and they brought me two gallon jugs of water, which came in handy.

Upon arriving at the hotel, a Marriott, I began to think about the logistics for the next day. The next day was a Sunday, and I wanted to go to Mass. When you have a car, going to Mass is nothing more than getting in the car and driving there. When you do not have a car, going to Mass in this case was a two-mile walk in each direction, and that was before I would be starting my thirty-two miles planned for the day.

To put it in perspective, walking the distance back and forth to Mass, four miles total, at my speed was almost an hour and a half, which would be on top of the time needed to get the miles in for the day. That reality hit hard that night.

March 16, 2014

> *What an absolutely amazing day. First it is so kind all the words you all are saying. Please remember though I'm doing this as a walk of atonement as well as gratitude. It was very important to me that this walk not be about me but about the children. It is one of the reasons why I want to talk about issues I ran into during the walk because it reinforces the wonderful nature of people and how our Savior has touched so many of us particularly me. That is why it is a walk of gratitude as well.*

I met so many amazing people today.

Mike Burrell not only offered to drive me to Mass but also held some of my gear while I walked the next twenty miles. He then delivered it to me later in the day. You have to keep in mind that Mike is from Phoenix, Arizona, and we were in San Diego. He was offering to do this out of the kindness of his heart.

Think about what Mike did. Mike drove me to Mass and then, an hour later, picked me up and took me back to the hotel. At the hotel, he coordinated with me, Joyce, and Monique to take the gear that I would not need for the day's walk and delivered it to me twenty miles later. At the same time, Joyce and Monique were so kind to take me to the start point from where I ended the day before. All this was done without any advance planning, and I believe it was by the hand of God that it happened at all.

Life Lessons Learned: **Have faith! Trust in our Savior and His mother.**

Put in perspective, if Jan, Mike, Monique, and Joyce had not been willing to help, I would have had to walk a total of four miles to Mass and then another six miles to get back to the prior day's start point to continue a journey. In other words, I would have walked almost ten miles and not covered any ground at all.

Trust became a theme that influenced me personally in profound ways. I had to trust Mike, and I had to trust Joyce and Monique. I wanted to trust them, but I actually *had* to trust them. There is a huge difference between wanting to trust and having to trust.

Life Lessons Learned: **People are genuinely decent. Have trust.**

I had no choice. If they did not offer to help, I probably would have shed some of my gear or left it at a hotel, went to Mass, and hoped the gear was there when I got back.

I had to trust, which meant I had to have faith that they would be willing to help me even though they did not know me. I began to think at this point and for the rest of the journey how kind, compassionate, and wonderful people are. I began to ask myself if I would have done the same thing. I think I would have, but I wondered.

A logical question is why I did the logistics the way I did. Attempting to have a daily mileage goal was counterproductive, as I was to find out immediately. It was a major flaw in the planning process in which I made achieving some many miles per day the goal rather than looking at the locations where I was walking.

If I had to do it again or if I were to advise anyone else, I would encourage them to make the terrain and sleeping locations the major determining factor in determining how many miles covered per day. The miles-per-day syndrome was a training phenomenon that was unrealistic for this journey.

Fortunately, my shortsightedness in walk planning taught me the lesson I believe God wanted me to learn, and that was to have trust and to have faith. My mistake and error in planning taught me perhaps the greatest lesson of all.

At Mass, Father John blessed all the petitions. His words of encouragement were heartfelt and brought a tear to this old man's eyes. Father John's beautiful words to me to encourage me on my journey were so touching. He wrote in my journal:

God is with you in every step of your journey.

Joyce and Monique from the Deltas were simply phenomenal, a Delta trend that would continue throughout the walk. I caused quite a scare when they thought that I was missing while I was at Mass.

The motherly devotion of Joyce and Monique and the scare that I must have caused them when they thought that perhaps I had collapsed in my room just reinforced to me how wonderful a feeling it was to know that someone cared. Learning this message this early in the walk was a great reflection of the motherly love that the Sisters of the Good Shepherd have for our children and that our Blessed Mother has for each and every one of us.

Life Lessons Learned: **Care about one another.**

Jan Jensen arrived at the end of the day as she promised. She made certain she picked me up on the outskirts of Julian, California, took me to the hotel, and made arrangements to have someone pick me up in the morning to take me back to where I left off. What a wonderful lady!

What was astonishing about what Jan did was that she showed genuine care and concern for someone she did not even know and then brought her entire network of friends to help a total stranger. Her kindness stunned me. I would read newspapers and watch TV and see nothing but distress and pain in the world, and yet so far, I had seen nothing but kindness and compassion. I was not quite sure what to make of that just yet.

Life Lessons Learned: **Look for the best in people and treat them with kindness.**

Less than forty-eight hours earlier, I was at sea level, and by the end of the second day, I was almost at four thousand feet up. What a climb! Walking up hills did not bother me at all, and in fact, I found it exhilarating.

Earlier in the day, when I was leaving the hotel in San Diego, I misplaced my walking stick, which had been given as a gift to me by my marines when I was a battalion commander in training in Quantico, Virginia. The walking stick meant a great deal to me, but I also needed it. I was not able to replace it until I got to Brawley, California. You cannot imagine how important it is to have a walking stick when you are going downhill. It is nice to have going uphill, but it is essential to have going downhill.

I began using a walking stick during my training for this walk. It is amazing what a simple piece of wood can do to help.

Life Lessons Learned: **The greatest gifts are sometimes the simplest.**

A dear friend, Doug Sethness, who was to join me later for three days, sent me kind words when he knew I was having some concerns about my stamina. The physical demands were substantial, but so were the emotional ones. I had someone send me a message in the morning of the second day in which they said I had almost completed 1 percent of the journey. That message was definitely well-intentioned, but what a jolt. I learned to joke about it later, but the comment was a stark reminder that I was only at the beginning.

By the second day, I was getting overwhelmed by being behind schedule. I realized that I was not yet acclimated to the temperature and had not yet completed 1 percent of the walk. To have someone remind me that I was not yet at 1 percent of the walk yet feeling the way that I did almost demotivated me rather than motivated me.

Diana Ellis would occasionally joke with me when I would tell her that I have completed another five miles to remind me that I only had twelve million more steps to do. We both laughed.

The ability to laugh and have others laugh helped me realize that we can make this journey together. I had no idea that how I felt today would be the best I would feel for the next sixty days!

Life Lessons Learned: **Laugh hard. Laugh often.**

March 17, 2014

> *On the road again! Encourage you to think of me singing that! :-)*

Keeping a sense of humor was a key part of the entire walk but especially at the beginning of the journey.

The value of having a sense of humor was essential to keeping the positive energy and a positive attitude that were needed to cross this beautiful nation of ours.

When I was on my way to Julian, California, I saw a sign that said Entering Cleveland National Forest. Keep in mind that I had only gone about sixty miles at this point but could not help but start laughing. I even sent out the Facebook note that said, "I'm either making really good progress or I made one heck of a wrong turn!"

I just could not resist! The comment allowed me to laugh a little, which I needed to do in light of the fact that my feet were beginning to feel the effects of having walked sixty miles with a fifty-pound backpack and pushing a seventy- to eighty-pound cart. Not that it was difficult. It was just the shock effect from not having trained extensively in the first three months before leaving on March 15. This was where the effects of not considering the impact of weather on training were felt.

As I was praying for all my special intentions, I had time to think about the logistics of what I was doing, the way we structured the journey, and how we might need to make a midcourse correction.

The original intent was that I would just find the support along the way and rely on the good graces of so many people. I found that was possible to do, and we were able to stick with that part of the plan for the first ten days, but then I began to feel guilty about how much I was putting people out by my requests. People were willing to do it, but I felt that was wrong of me to expect it.

In particular, what the Deltas had done and what John and Cynthia Lovewell, Jan Jensen, Mike Burrell, and others had done for me felt as if it were above and beyond the call of duty and I was not being fair to ask them to go that much out of their way.

I began to think there had to be a better way to do what I was doing, and with the help of Diana Ellis and Joe Simmers, a dear friend of mine from home and then a lieutenant in the Marine Corps, we were able to craft a solution that allowed me to do the walk while minimizing the inconvenience of other people.

As I was climbing from sea level in San Diego to over 4,300 feet in Julian, California, I thought I was beginning the walk up to heaven. I posted on Facebook, "Apparently I'm beginning to think that looking up to heaven means I have to climb up to it! :-)"

During the first few days, and it was a trend that continued throughout, I received words of encouragement. One in particular that really touched me was a message from Sister Mary Catherine, with whom I worked at Good Shepherd Services.

> *God bless you Frank, we are wrapping you in prayer.*

> *Sr. Mary Catherine*

The constant encouragement that I received from the sisters was so helpful. I wish you can know the Sisters of the Good Shepherd the way I do. I have yet to meet anyone as humble and as kind as they are. Every time I tried to pay the sisters a compliment, they deflected it back, because to them, humility and service are what they live by. The idea of giving personal accolades to a sister is a concept totally foreign to them.

I wanted very much to emulate the sisters' attitude during this walk to make sure that people knew that the walk was a walk of atonement and gratitude on my part. I often said that if I had not sinned, I would not need to do a walk of atonement. It was important that the focus was for it to be an endeavor for our children and to atone for my past sins.

During the walk today, I climbed about 1,400 feet in elevation. The lesson that I learned was what it means to depend on other people. I used to think that being in control was extremely important, when in fact, being in control is a major problem. We have to be able to trust in order for us to have faith, because Christ will provide. Just look at the beautiful landscape that God has provided for us. I also found out today that it is possible for a blister on a blister!

Life Lessons Learned: **Allow others to help you. Accept assistance graciously and gratefully.**

It was interesting to get to the point of realizing that I had to trust. I think today was the day I came to believe that I had to have faith that Christ would lead me through this journey. I had a very positive attitude all day and was actually buoyed by the understanding that I was not in control. That was the first time I really felt what those words meant. That is a unique concept to "feel a meaning" of something. It was the first time it happened to me.

Life Lessons Learned: **Empathy requires us to feel how others feel, to care.**

I welcomed comments on Facebook and especially the e-mails that I received from Greg Conderacci, particularly his words of wisdom. The comments reinforced the understanding of the importance of human contact and how important that must be for our children.

Today I received a very nice message from Kim Rust, who works with my brother-in-law. Kim said, "Frank, thirty years ago, our church had a ministry to Good Shepherd Center. We would take homemade treats and spend time with the girls, sometimes doing crafts and sign language lessons. Our church had a strict "no dancing" policy, but I remember going to the Center and the wife of one of our deacons getting up and dancing with the girls."

Seeing how Kim's church helped so many years ago and the impact it must have had on those children reinforced the message of human care and concern.

When I posted on Facebook that I was joking that I had blisters on blisters, I received a nice comment from my friend Ann. I wrote back to her and said,

> *Ann actually I was surprised. I haven't had a blister in over a year. I think it's the fact that I'm in the mountains and I'm using the ball of my foot more which is where the blisters developed. It's all good though as long as I don't stop! :-). Compared to what our children go through it's not a concern at all. You're going to be in my prayers as well my friend.*

The feeling I was starting to experience with my feet while at the same time knowing I can stop at any time gave me great comfort. I could not help but think what it must be like for our children and the parents of our children when they do not know when the end is.

***Life Lessons Learned*: Hope builds lives. Despair destroys lives.**

When I realized later that I was not going to complete the walk on time and did not know when I was going to be done, I felt for the first time, in a very small way, what our children and the parents of our children must feel. I needed to feel that feeling. Feeling the meaning of something became part of who I am, so I can understand how to help more.

My niece, actually the wife of my nephew, Karin, was curious about the route I was taking, so I sent her this response:

> *Karin I'm walking predominately on the roads. Still getting used to the altitude and temperatures. Miss all of you guys. Got all of my prayer requests in for you, your parents, and*

your family as well as the little cherubs. Please tell my sister
Pat that I love her and that I miss her and will call her
soon as I get back. I am praying for her.

This was important to me not only to let Karin know that I was
thinking of her but also to have her tell my sister Pat that I love her. Pat
was starting to require long-term care, and all I thought about was how
Pat sacrificed so much of her childhood to help raise my sister Gene and
myself. Pat's caring was instrumental in my life.

March 18, 2014

The day started with a Mass in Julian, where I met many wonderful
people. Father was so gracious. I met with him and some other fellow
parishioners after Mass for coffee and a time of fellowship. This was one
of the few times that I found that Father had expected my visit from the
letter that the bishop of San Diego had sent out, asking for assistance
while I was walking. It was a very heartwarming gesture.

During the travels for the day, I traveled twenty-two miles from Julian
and descended about four thousand feet during the process as I entered
the desert. I was shocked by the number of people who stopped me in
the desert and asked me if I needed assistance.

The drop from Julian, California, to the desert stunned me a little, and
I had a powerful learning experience from it. I was using a cart, and
during the descent, I realized that while walking downhill with a fifty-
pound backpack (meaning I had full forward momentum), I had to,
at the same time, pull back on the cart to make sure that I did not lose
control of all my gear. The scenery was so gorgeous that I had no idea,
until I got to the bottom of the hill, that my feet were absorbing all the
friction of going downhill while pulling back on a cart. At the bottom
of the mountain (four thousand feet, mind you), I took my socks off to
change them and found my feet absolutely raw! The blisters had burst,
the socks were bloodied, and the pain was excruciating once I took the
shoes off and released that pressure. Ouch!

Today was the first day that I was outside of any cell phone coverage for
an extended period. I was in the middle of the desert! At first I thought

the isolation was a little scary, but after a few minutes—and I literally mean a few minutes—I began to embrace the new experience. I was on my own, or was I? I would find out in the hours ahead that I was constantly being protected by the Most Holy Trinity and the Blessed Mother of our Savior. Not bad company!

Life Lessons Learned: **We are never alone, if we believe!**

Despite all the discomfort, the scenery was so beautiful, and I was so isolated that I did not mind it. Once I got done for the night though, I realized what I had done and needed the sleep time to get my feet bandaged. What a day.

My inexperience with using the equipment, in not having a brake on the cart, and in hitting the mountains so quickly all contributed to what could have been a disaster. This was the first time that I began to question whether or not I was going to make the journey. It was a very sobering time.

I also got my first flat tire! It was in the middle of the desert, and I did not have a spare with me. I mistakenly thought that I would get about 250 miles out of the tires and planned on resupplying in Brawley. The flat occurred about forty miles from Brawley. I was able to continue with the flat until I was picked up at the end of the day by a fellow friend from Cornwall, Pennsylvania, Joe Simmers, and his wife, Allison.

The significance of the help of Joe and Allison cannot be overstated. Their kindness and generosity overwhelmed me, to say the least. I did not appreciate at the time I called Joe to ask for his assistance of the distances what I was putting him and Allison through. They were in Yuma, Arizona, and I was walking from Julian, California, toward Brawley.

The distances are almost 150 miles from Yuma to where I was, and both Joe and Allison were incredibly helpful and willing to assist. I did not realize how much I put them out until I had gotten to Yuma five or six days later.

To do this for a friend was more than anyone can reasonably expect, and they did it with complete joy in their hearts. I often wondered if I would do the same. I believe I would, but there was that lingering doubt, a doubt that I will no longer have because this is a walk of atonement and gratitude.

Life Lessons Learned: **Give gifts unconditionally.**

This incident encouraged me to think about what I was putting the staff at Good Shepherd through during the beginning stages of the walk, most particularly Diana Ellis.

I did not realize it at that time, but when I started walking and was trying to arrange logistics simultaneously with walking the no-call zones and no-cell-phone-coverage areas, it made advanced planning difficult, so I had to rely on Diana to help me find support and areas to stay.

This was a mistake in the advanced planning on my part. I did not fully appreciate the distances between cities and towns. This combination of factors and the fact that I was not familiar with the area set the stage for incredible demands being placed on people not able to the experience what I was currently dealing with.

Fortunately, by this part of the trip, I was convinced that no matter what, God has a solution. I did not necessarily need to learn that lesson anymore, nor did I need to burden anyone else with an ill-conceived plan, so I began to think of logistics issues differently. By the time I got to Brawley and in talking with Joe Simmers, I began to reformulate the logistics plan.

The time in the desert was fantastic. The beauty and serenity were overwhelming. It was a great time to pray and reflect. The temperatures were already into the midnineties, but even that was relatively comfortable because I was so mesmerized.

It was almost two days before I realized the potential problem with my isolation and some of the coyotes near me. I would come to understand shortly what coyotes were really about.

I had time to reflect on how many wonderful people there are in this nation and that this walk of atonement and gratitude is a spiritual journey of a lifetime and an opportunity to help our children in getting the care that they need.

I learned a great deal so far on this trip about myself. I love to do as much as I can to help people, but sometimes I find that I just do not have enough time. One of the things that I said was that this walk of atonement was for people that I have disappointed, so that they would pray for me. The great support that I have seen so far and the dangers to my health if people had not been able to help as promised only reinforced my need to make sure that I was able to make my commitments. I promised to do better. This had been the most concentrated time to reflect I have ever had.

If you have ever let someone down, please give them a call and tell them you are sorry.

Life Lessons Learned: **Only say yes when you intend to help and are able to help. Unfilled promises are hurtful.**

Life Lessons Learned: **It is very important to tell someone you have disappointed or hurt them, that you are sorry—and mean it.**

March 19, 2014

In the morning, Paul Funez from the Knights of Columbus in Brawley picked me up and took me to the prior day's end point. From Brawley to that start point was almost forty minutes, so it was a tremendous inconvenience for Paul. He was so gracious to be so accommodating.

By the fifth day of the trip, my feet were unbelievably sensitive. Actually, they just plain hurt. I was limping from the discomfort and from the blisters that covered the entire bottom of my feet. The temperatures were approaching one hundred degrees. But I had to keep my sense of humor.

While walking, I saw a hubcap that someone had painted to look like a flying saucer. I took a picture of the hubcap and sent out this Facebook note: "Had a very close call. I'm safe now. Aliens on this spacecraft almost got me.:-)"

I thought it was really funny, but apparently, my humor was directly related to the discomfort I was feeling, since my Facebook supporters apparently did not see the picture the same way I did.

The desert landscape was simply breathtaking. I was out of cell phone range and out of contact for about six hours yesterday and today while in the desert between Julian and Brawley.

I received so many well-wishes and prayers when I was out of range. I prayed for all those who cared for our children and for all our children.

Our walk took me out of San Diego County finally and led me into Imperial County, California. I was one hundred miles into our trek.

I saw firsthand the power of prayer! Fortunately, when I was training, I trained to get myself to the point of heat exhaustion so that I would know how to prevent or recover if necessary. At about seven hours into the trip, the temperatures approached one hundred degrees, and I could feel heat exhaustion coming on. There was no place to go for cover, and all the water that I had was heated from the weather even though I had it undercover.

There was no one around. I was isolated. I knew I was in trouble. So I did the only thing that I knew to do, and that was to pray. I asked our Blessed Mother to intercede for me with her son, our Savior, and provide me with a cool breeze so that I could cool down. Literally seconds later, a cool breeze came out from the west and cooled me off quickly. After I cooled off a little from the breeze, it dawned on me that I could take the hot water and pour it onto the scarf I was wearing to cool down my neck. That worked wonders.

I could not help but laugh that my prayer was answered so quickly, so I teasingly looked up into heaven and asked the Blessed Mother if she could send me a few Snickers bars. I then pretended to cover my head from the lightning and just started to laugh.

I had my first major test of my resolve today as well. A young man and his son stopped near me, and I offered to take their picture as I was resting. They were trying to take a selfie. We started talking about the walk and about me being a retired marine, when the father asked if I would like a ride to the Sultan Lake area about ten miles closer to the end of my daily trip. Keep in mind, I was really exhausted, but I was so thankful that our Savior guided me to do the right thing, which was to say that I just needed to keep walking.

The father was relieved, because at first, he told me that no one would know if I took a ride. I said the only person that really mattered would know, and that was our Savior. He was genuinely pleased with my comment. It was a very touching moment. I was very thankful that I did not succumb to this first temptation.

Life Lessons Learned: **Avoid temptation. The end does not justify the means.**

I was very fortunate to be picked up by Paul Funez that evening. He took me to the hotel in Brawley for the night.

We had an outstanding meeting with the Knights of Columbus in Brawley, California. With such great knights, our world is in a better place. They were the unsung heroes of the journey.

March 20, 2014

Paul picked me up in the morning to continue back in the desert. I saw firsthand the problems that Mexican Americans had near the border. The illegal alien issue was such a problem.

Since we were so close to the Mexican border, there were border control points that we had to cross going from Brawley past Sultan Lake and back into the desert. Because Paul was of Mexican descent, he was stopped and questioned more frequently, particularly because he made multiple trips back and forth in the desert to pick me up and drop me off.

What the border patrol was apparently looking for was the pattern of going back and forth into the desert, so on the last trip, they detained Paul at the border patrol checkpoint while they had an agent check on me in the desert to confirm Paul's story. Keep in mind that Paul is a US citizen.

I talked to Paul, his wife, Rosie, and his friends about the issue, and they put a different perspective on this problem than I had considered before.

They mentioned that the area where they lived was an ancestral home for their families, meaning that it predated the founding of the United States. It was not uncommon for families in what is now the United States to have cousins in what is now Mexico.

The other issue they mentioned, as did the border patrol, was that federal government social policies complicated the problem. For instance, in the desert, a watering hole was set up to provide water for those people crossing the desert so they did not die from heat stroke and dehydration. To preclude the illegal alien from feeling threatened with arrest at these locations, border patrol agents were not permitted near the watering hole.

Unfortunately, the altruistic motive of providing a safe haven for water actually put the illegal immigrant in greater danger. The danger came from the "coyote."

Prior to this discussion, my idea of coyote meant the animal, but I found out very quickly that the coyote was the person who was getting paid to get people across the border. Since the safe haven was created at the watering hole, the coyote was free to abuse the illegal alien and put that person into slavery of varying sorts within the United States. That slavery includes prostitution and child slavery.

I came to learn about coyotes more than I ever dreamed about in the next two weeks when local police and border patrol agents gently cautioned me that I too was at risk from the coyote looking to ransom me to my family. I had no idea this was going on in the United States.

This incident and the incidents in the following weeks gave me a reality check to always look for unintended consequences. I questioned what we were doing with programs for our children and the potential unintended consequences of what we were doing to help. Just because we thought it helped does not mean that it in fact does help.

Life Lessons Learned: **Always look for unintended consequences of your actions.**

This concern about what really works for our children became a recurring theme for my entire walk. I have become convinced that for us to help children, we must always be willing to critically challenge the assumptions under which we operate.

I was certain that the core values of my faith and the core values of the Sisters of the Good Shepherd and Saint Mary Euphrasia were rock solid, but how we implemented those core values and beliefs systems were what needed to be critically analyzed and challenged.

Throughout this part of the walk, the border patrol was so decent and professional. At the one checkpoint, they allowed me to sit in a shaded area as I continued my journey through the desert. I met a former marine there as well.

Some of the scenes that were particularly fascinating for me included the bridges over dry gullies in the desert. From my experiences at Twentynine Palms and in desert training in the Marine Corps as well as in Iraq and Afghanistan, I knew all too well what those dry gullies really meant.

Whenever it would rain in some far-off distance in the mountains surrounding this desert, these dry creek beds became flooded almost instantly and could be quite dangerous.

Today I started to come out of the desert. I was on my way into the Imperial Valley. In the distance, you could see the Sultan Lake. I had a great deal of time to think about the special intentions everyone had asked me to pray, such as Bud Werner.

I mentioned Bud because many people asked me to pray for a specific person on a specific day for a reason that they either did or did not share with me. When someone asked me to pray on a certain day, I tried to take a picture of the area where I was when I was saying the prayers. I then send the photo to the person, asking for the prayers for their special intention. Many times the significance of the photo was only known to God and the person who asked me to say a prayer. It was a nice feeling to know that we can honor someone in that way.

In crossing into the Imperial Valley, I was beginning to realize that it had already taken me from the fifteenth to the twentieth just to get out of San Diego County, and I was not through California yet. I made that comment to a friend of mine who let me know that the distance I had already gone was like crossing Connecticut. Since I spent a lot of time in Rhode Island, Connecticut, and Massachusetts, I had to chuckle, because distances on the East Coast are significantly different than distances on the West Coast. Little did I know that crossing Arizona and New Mexico would reinforce that learning point.

***Life Lessons Learned*: Perspectives are different based on our own experiences.**

It was a rough day! I completed twenty-three miles, but it took me nine and a half hours to do it. I slowed down due to some equipment failures and, reluctantly I have to admit, age. The prayers that you sent were appreciated. Those prayers helped me keep focused on looking at our children and not thinking too much about how I was feeling at the moment.

Tomorrow is a light-training day to recuperate, and then I head back out again on Saturday morning to the full-training mode twenty to twenty-five miles each day. Once I get acclimated, I am hoping that I can increase the mileage beyond that.

The scenery is magnificent. I am having dinner in Brawley tonight with some friends. I find Brawley to be one of the wealthiest towns in America because they cherish their families and their children. Wealth is not about money but about caring for one another. I found many such towns in California already.

I had a chance to have a great meal with great friends. Due to the efforts of fellow board member Will Butterazzi and the kindness of Paul and Rosie Funez, we had dinner with members of the Knights of Columbus in Brawley.

I am so grateful for the chance to meet so many wonderful people during this trip, particularly some newfound friends from Brawley, California. The Blessed Mother and our Savior gave me the greatest gift during this trip: friends, both at home and here in California.

Each day I received a nice passage, poem, or wise saying or expression from Greg. Those comments made me feel very special and cared about, and I would encourage you to do that with those in your life. You may never know the impact that a kind word or caring concern may have.

Life Lessons Learned: **A simple act of caring may be the greatest gift you will ever receive or give.**

March 21, 2014

A dear friend, Laura LeBeau, asked me to pray for her mom and dad during my walk. I can think of no better day to do that than on her birthday. Happy birthday, Laura. I sent Laura a picture of what I was looking at when I was praying for her mom and dad.

I stopped for the day after nine miles for recuperation and planning. Tomorrow, I am heading to Yuma, Arizona, and have been thinking a great deal about the logistics of the walk and would appreciate your prayers as we replan.

Some of the things that I needed to replan included the miles per day as well as the logistics of getting from one point to another. It was very clear to me at this point that I was not going to be able to do the thirty-two miles per day that I hoped for. My physical limitations and the number of days that I knew I was going to be walking were now going to be well over one hundred days.

I also realized that I was truly inconveniencing people. It was selfish on my part to try to ask people to help me in the way I was trying to do it, so I began to think of alternative ways to resolve the problem and to be considerate of others while getting the message out. This driving back and forth, which was necessitated so that I could meet people and talk to them about our mission, also inadvertently created a horrible imposition on people that were willing to do it, but I had no right to ask them to do it.

The first week was coming to a close. We did about 130 miles for the week. We did approximately two miles for each year of my age. I was joking a little bit about the fact that at one spot in Brawley, I was about one hundred feet below sea level, which was one hundred feet below where I started from in San Diego but that it sure did not feel that way. I started at zero or sea level and climbed to 4,400 feet in Julian, California, and was now below where I started. I just could not help but see the humor in that!

The most important thing I have learned this week, though, is the goodness and kindness of people for one another. I am positive that we can solve this problem of providing and caring for developmentally disabled children. Our effort must be based upon compassion, love for children, and long-term needs of families.

I was struck by the kindness and generosity of so many people this week. There were people who had no idea of who I was and did not care who I was other than being a human being who had a need. I was at a restaurant, for example, at the end of the training week. A person who worked there offered to pay for my lunch. When I declined, she insisted. I saw the sincerity in her eyes and connected immediately with her as one human to another. She allowed me to tell the Good Shepherd story to others.

I decided to present a medallion of the Good Shepherd Sisters to her. Our mission is to care for the most abandoned soul.

When she showed the medallion to her coworker, I explained to the coworker what we were trying to do. When I mentioned to her, for example, about a parents of children with Down syndrome, worrying about what will happen to their children should they pass away, the coworker almost cried. She said that is similar to her situation with one of her grandchildren.

She encouraged me to continue getting the message out.

I mentioned to Betty, who asked me a question on the blog about my route, that I should be in Twentynine Palms by late tomorrow or early Sunday. I had to do a hop, skip, and jump around some road issues due to construction and limited-access highways. I planned on making up the miles that I was rerouted outside of Yuma. It turned out there were parts of this area that were a "no man's" land relative to construction and safety.

March 22, 2014

A dear friend of mine, Toni Gilhooley, sent me a note of encouragement on Facebook. I told Toni that I said a rosary for her and Bill and asked her to keep fighting the good fight so we can make this world a better place for all. I really appreciated her words of encouragement.

Another friend of mine on Facebook by the name of Beth asked me to keep her father and her in my prayers since he passed away recently. She missed him dearly. In my note back to her, I said, "Beth you know who you are and this is the scene I was looking at when I was praying for your dad and you. God bless you both."

I also had the chance to walk to the top of an extinct volcano at the Salton Sea.

I am so impressed with the generosity of those I have seen and met on this trip. I am heading into Arizona this evening. I had the opportunity to spend some time with Andrew, who was going into the Franciscans. Andrew was a very young man and a very faithful human being who has a tremendous desire to serve our Savior. I met him through Paul and Rosie, and I am thankful that they made the introduction.

It is wonderful to see the dedication and faith of so many young people.

One of the things that really struck me was this flagpole in Calipatria, California, that is 184 feet below sea level, and the top of the flagpole has been deliberately set to be at sea level. The town of Brawley itself is 113 feet below sea level. There is an unbelievable amount of geothermal activity here. What I was most impressed with was the series of water canals that come from the Colorado River, the absence of which would turn this entire area into a desert rather than as a food basket.

Life Lessons Learned: Without blood, man will not survive. Without water, mankind will not survive.

I was never a big fan of avocados until I came to this part of California. Here, I found them to be absolutely tasty and delightful, and I was becoming a huge fan in only a few days. But the reality of how vulnerable the area was to its water supply became very apparent to me. The water issue was not just here but all the way into Kansas. This whole region had been in a horrific drought. The area was so dependent upon water flow from the Colorado River.

The water dependency made me appreciate the vulnerability that all of us have to factors outside of our control. The immensity of the area where I was walking and the realization of our vulnerability reinforced my faith that God is in control and not us!

Life Lessons Learned: **God is in control—surrender and trust.**

We completed over twenty miles today. I had to make major revisions to the plans for safety reasons. I am currently staying in Yuma with marine friends Joe and Allison Simmers, whom I considered to be one of the unsung heroes of this trip.

March 23, 2014

Today I began walking in Yuma, Arizona.

I was getting an entirely different insight into the issues about drug cartels and the control that they have on America than I ever imagined. There are more social problems created by this drug problem, but what I would love to see is what can be done to resolve the crisis and to get to the root cause of the use of illegal drugs. Many of the problems we deal with in our children are drug related.

Joe Simmers recommended I try a new product called coconut water. The thought of that did not appeal to me, but I trusted Joe. What a great product! This coconut water helps absorb potassium quickly, which is absolutely essential to survival.

I somewhat forgot how important potassium is, particularly when you are drinking a great deal of water. If your potassium level drops, your energy dissipates quickly, and when you are my age, you also put your health, particularly your heart health, at risk.

I was stopping to get a bite to eat, and I ran into two extremely polite, decent, respectful folks. It turned out they were both United States Marines! They represented New York and Texas. Both of their families should be extraordinarily proud. I know the Marine Corps family is. God bless them both.

In the Marine Corps, we always stress the brotherhood that we all have with all marines and their families. This brotherhood lasts forever, and that is why you hear the expression there is no such thing as an ex-marine. We will always stand to help one another.

In much the same way, Good Shepherd Services is trying to rebuild the family structure for many of our children and help their families deal with the issues that they have. A healthy family environment is essential for our children. That sounds counterintuitive, but there are unhealthy "family" structures, such as gangs, that attempt to replicate the family that can be destructive. These are all the types of issues that I am hoping this walk will allow us to concentrate on so we can develop a meaningful solution to help our children with behavioral, emotional, and developmental disabilities.

Life Lessons Learned: **Family and friends are so important. Cherish them and let them know you care.**

My times are slowing down a little bit as I continue to get acclimated to the different climate and walking. The blisters and swelling in the feet are slowing me down although I am getting used to it. My physical issues remind me that while I can stop when I am hurting, our children who are developmentally disabled cannot control their situation, so we have to create a safe place for all of them. May we forever cherish the wonderful charge that we have in caring for children.

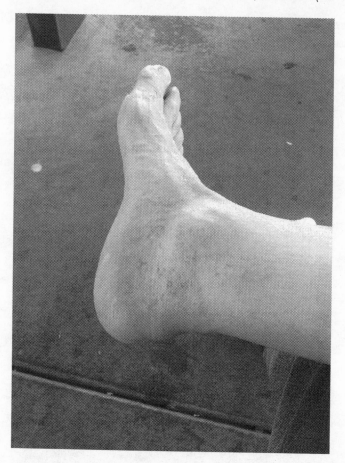

I mention about the ability to stop at any time because that has become a recurring source of comfort for me while I am walking. For someone facing an emotional or behavioral problem, that situation is not voluntary. In other words, it was comforting to me to know that my decisions are voluntary, but when someone is suffering with any other type of problem, it may not be. Imagine feeling out of control all the time!

I heard from a dear friend of mine today, Lin and Jerry Shenk. Lin said, "Thinking of you, Frank. You are in my prayers. Thank you so very much for your rosary prayer for my mother. I know it reached her. We are keeping track of you on your journey to help the kids at Good Shepherd. Godspeed, my friend. Lin (Jerry, too)." What a nice message from home!

We have completed a total of twenty miles and have done a total so far of 172 miles. Today I had a chance to reflect on a number of things. I talked to so many wonderful people who have been so engaged and thoughtful as we strive to solve problems for our children.

Being passionate is so incredibly important. I would encourage you to find the cause for which you are as passionate about as I am about Good Shepherd and decide to make a difference.

Life Lessons Learned: **Be passionate about life.**

It has been a humbling week to see how helpful everyone has been to a total stranger. I witnessed firsthand many miracles.

March 24, 2014

Today is a very special day for me. My walk is a walk of gratitude, and today is my sister Pat's birthday. Pat was twelve years old when our dad died. I was three and a half, and my sister Genie was six months old. On that day, Pat and my brothers Ed and Bob lost their childhood after Dad died because they were thrown into becoming caretakers of the younger brother (that would be me) and younger sister. They, like my mom and grandmother, sacrificed everything so that Genie and I had a normal childhood.

For my sister Patty Lou, I remembered how much she has sacrificed for others. Her sacrifices made every day of my life the absolute best. Thank you, Patty Lou!

We completed over twenty miles today. I left Joe and Allyson Simmers this morning and walked to Yuma before heading off to the east. I made it to Wellton, Arizona, when I was pulled over by a sheriff. It was the fourth time that happened since the journey started. The officer was a deputy sheriff from Yuma County. He was very much interested in the reasons for the walk and how important it was to come up with a solution to help our children.

The folks here are just as interested in making sure that people are safe. He mentioned to me that they normally do not see people walking where I was walking. He wanted to make sure I was okay. He told me about a monk that he saw about two weeks earlier who was walking across the desert for prayer.

March 25, 2014

I started the day with a wonderful message from a good friend, Pam Devine. I have always been impressed by Pam's integrity and her positive outlook on life.

From Pam Devine:

> *Thought of you this morning as I ran in stark contrast to your walk. A short COLD run as opposed to your LONG HOT walk. Just as I was about to quit it started to snow. A sure sign from the heavens that you are being taken care of . . . and motivating me to do one more mile. Thinking of you the whole way.*

After reading a few comments on the blog, I headed to Mass to pray for our children.

In the blogs, friends would ask me to take selfies, but I am not comfortable having my picture taken. So I took a picture of my shadow, and I said, "Have you all noticed that since I started this walk I have gotten taller? When I went for my last physical, my doctor told me my weight was fine but I was 4 inches too short. I'm very happy to announce that I think I've solved the shortness problem! :-)."

The need to keep a sense of humor was important, and it made the day go by quickly. I am convinced that a positive attitude is critical for everyone. I jokingly told all my friends at the beginning of the trip that I was going to be spending a lot of time with myself and I certainly hoped that by the end of the trip, I still liked me.

Life Lessons Learned: It is very difficult to love others if you do not like yourself.

While I made that comment in jest, it was all too true, because you really do get to know yourself quite well when you spend a great deal of time alone to reflect. The walk of atonement was working.

I start back walking tomorrow after taking a day to recuperate. I will be doing twenty miles per day for the rest of this week and then hope to step it up to twenty-five miles per day. The primary mission of this walk is to get the word out about the needs of children with behavioral and emotional difficulties.

While I am hoping to make up the mileage that I am behind on, I do have time after July 1 to get caught up. This has been the biggest challenge for me. I am trying to recognize that it is God's schedule and not mine. In this "down" day to get laundry done and recuperate, I have had the chance to meet more people and talk about our missions than I ever dreamed of. Perhaps that was Christ's plan to begin with.

Life Lessons Learned: **Do not try to control those things you cannot.**

I often wonder what I have overlooked in my life, because I have been so busy that I failed to see what is really important. Follow your heart and your faith!

During my walk, Brian, who was working with the Maryland Association of CPAs, completed seven video updates, and Bill Sheridan of the MACPA did an interview about the walk as well. It was a chance to talk with friends back home and get the message out about what the walk was like. About ten days into the walk, Bill Sheridan and I talked, and this is what he wrote in his blog.

> *Just spoke with Frank Ryan 10 days into his Walk Across America. The short version: A few obstacles aside, he's doing great! Update to come on the Maryland Association of CPAs' blog, CPA Success.*

March 26, 2014

I started back on the walk this morning! I started bright and early to try to get a head start on the heat. It was still dark, and in the distance,

I saw a light. I did not know what it was. It did not seem to be getting any closer, and I did not hear anything. But I quickly found out that that light in the distance was a train. The distances in the desert are deceiving, and so are speeds.

What a great day! The day started with a twelve-mile hike in Wellton, Arizona, and ended with multiple short hikes of nine miles each up to Chandler, Arizona, to meet with great friends from the Delta Sigma Theta Sorority.

We put into effect a major change in the way we did the logistics for the walk. I found that walking from San Diego to Brawley, California, not having a support vehicle put an undue burden on those who are helping me. What I have decided to do is provide my own transportation for the very rural parts and park my car along the way to get most of the distances. Since there are some areas where that is not safe, such as about sixty miles between Yuma, Arizona, and Phoenix, I will have to make up for that around the surrounding areas of Phoenix. That same thing will happen between Phoenix and Albuquerque.

To make sure that I get the entire 2,806 miles, I decided to use MapMyWalk to track the mileage that I have done. This will confirm then that I have gotten all the mileage in. Once I get to the more populated areas, then we can go back to the original plan. The burden I have put on those supporting me is an unreasonable request for me to expect.

This change was a major hurdle for me to accept, because I wanted to complete the journey as I originally planned. I finally had to come to the realization that I had some major flaws in my planning for this trip.

Life Lessons Learned: **Deal with obstacles. Do not ignore them. Bad news does not get better with time.**

There were two major planning flaws that necessitated the change. First, I had multiple objectives that were mutually exclusive. Originally, my walk was a walk across United States as a walk of atonement and gratitude, which was a personal journey. Second, it became a walk to raise awareness of the needs of children with emotional, behavioral, and developmental disabilities.

The acceptance of this change in my plan actually convinced me that I had to accept my responsibility to the children first, and that was part of the atonement process.

Additionally, I realized that doing thirty-two miles per day rather than completing the journey between reasonable stopping points put me in a position of having to rely too much on outside, unplanned logistics for resupply.

In retrospect, it would have been much smarter to have a support vehicle if I had the type of plan that I did. By making the changes that I did, I was, in essence, providing my own support vehicle. This plan revision had some positive aspects and some negative ones that became apparent later on.

March 27, 2014

I had a little visitor this morning! I had my first encounter with a rattlesnake.

I was surprised that as much as I hate snakes, this did not bother me as much as I thought it would. I had about twenty incidents with snakes on the journey, and I realized quickly that when snakes are on the road, sunning, it is because they are cold, which means that they are not too agile. I got to the point by the end of the trip that snakes did not bother me at all.

There was a great six-mile hike this morning. Listening to the news at breakfast, I had heard about the firefighters in Boston and the little boy who lost his family in Darrington, Washington. Hearing the news like this made me appreciate having the time to pray for others.

We completed twenty miles for the day in four separate walks! I started walking between Yuma and Phoenix areas (great distance over multiple days) with stops in between in Gila Bend and Wellton. The police chief of Wellton and I talked for about twenty minutes about our mission and our walk. I have been incredibly impressed with all the folks from law enforcement that I have met here in Arizona.

The police chief was incredibly helpful, which reminded me of my own police chief, Chief Bruce Harris, in Cornwall, Pennsylvania. I am also learning the tremendous value of persistence and patience. Not a moment goes on this walk where I do not think about the suffering of children. That thought makes everything else seems very easy by comparison. I pray that I will always remain grateful, and I hope all of us will as well for the wonderful gifts we have been given. Joe and Alison Simmers are going to give me a ride back to Phoenix tomorrow so I can resume my walk under the revised plan.

Life Lessons Learned: **Be patient and be persistent. Stay the course.**

Comment from Karl Ahlrichs:

> *The pictures look great. It sounds like the new structure is working well.*
>
> *How ironic. For a few minutes, we're within a few miles of each other. I'm changing planes in Phoenix flying coast-to-coast in a few hours. You're taking far longer but more thoughtful track in the other direction.*

Karl is a great friend who has supported me with positive words and comments throughout the trip. Karl is a great photographer and a true inspiration.

March 28, 2014

Today was a logistics day of doing laundry and getting supplies. I dropped the rental car in Yuma and drove back to my Phoenix base for the next ten days to operate out of. This allowed me to stage some of my equipment so I was not carrying excess gear into the desert.

For my special intentions, I prayed the sorrowful mysteries of the rosary, and I ask all of you to consider the sacrifice and suffering that our Lord suffered and endured for our salvation. His sacrifice on the cross makes any discomfort that I am putting up with seem really mild in comparison. I hope that I always keep that in mind. We have so much to be thankful for always.

***Life Lessons Learned*: Christ died for our salvation!**

God works in mysterious ways! I want to be honest with you. I was getting a little cranky this evening from being so tired. I was praying that I would not be such a wimp. Letting minor things bother me is something I have to work on. With that in mind, I was trying to find a place to do my laundry, and it turned out it was about twenty-five minutes from where I was staying. When I was in the laundry, I met Brandon's dad, who explained that his son is autistic. When I told him what we were trying to do with our walk, his eyes teared up. It became apparent to both of us that we knew why this walk matters.

All of a sudden, the detour to the laundry made sense. The fact that I did not know the *why* the detour was of no consequence.

Brandon's dad and mom stayed in touch with me on Facebook for the rest of the journey, and I prayed for them daily. I would not have met them if the logistics did not take me so far away. It was all in God's plan. I just had to accept that.

March 29, 2014

Many things to think about today!

First, I was thinking about dogs. That's right, dogs. My son and daughter-in-law sent me a picture of George Washington Ryan, a Dalmatian puppy. He is living a life of leisure in the picture that they sent to me, and maybe we should learn that sometimes we should slow down as well.

Then I thought about faith and how important it is to believe. To believe is to trust, to trust is to have faith, and to have faith is to believe—the wonderful triangle of faith.

Life Lessons Learned: **To believe is to trust, to trust is to have faith, and to have faith is to believe—the triangle of faith.**

Finally, I met some incredibly wonderful people. One was Super Duper Cooper, as she called herself. She was so incredibly helpful and friendly, as was every person. While walking, I came across this fence on the bridge, and it reminded me of the fences that keep people in as much as the fences that keep people out, but in any perspective, it is still a barrier. I wondered how many times I let preconceived notions get in the way and become barriers to relationships. Think of all the wonderful people we could have met if defenses came down. Super Duper Cooper was breaking down barriers.

I wanted to close out the post for the day with a special prayer request for a dear friend. Her name is Diana Hester, and she passed away this past winter. Today was her fiftieth birthday. Another dear friend, Richard Boker, sent me a message today just to pray for Diana and reminded me that it was her birthday.

I told Richard, "Richard we said the Rosary of the Joyful mysteries today for Diana. The world was a better place because of Diana and we will all miss you. The CPA community was better because of her. So Diana we know you are in a better place now but your friends miss you dearly. This is what I was looking at when I was saying the prayers for Diana, Richard. God bless her!"

Life Lessons Learned: **Barriers work both ways: they keep people out, and they barricade you in.**

March 30, 2014

During the walk, I discovered many folks that were also considering walking such as this question.

> *Prayers to you along your journey. You are an inspiration to many. I'm Considering a walk myself this summer. Not quite as long only about 170 miles. Any advice?*

Before beginning my journey, many people referred me to websites of those who walked across America. The list appeared to be fairly short, but once I started walking, I realized that there have been thousands of people who have completed the same walk. They just did not have the means or perhaps the inclination to record it. Most of those who completed such a journey and recorded it usually did it for a cause, as I am doing.

When I responded, I was still fairly early into my journey. I mentioned to her that it was still very much of a learning experience for me, so my advice may be tempered by my lack of knowledge of what I was about to go into.

Life Lessons Learned: **Your advice is limited by your experiences. Everything that can be discovered has not yet been discovered.**

In much the same way, I find the same concerns relative to how we can best help children with problems. This is becoming a recurring theme and remained a recurring theme for my entire journey. We are framed by our experiences. We are hindered by our experiences. We are bettered by our experiences. We are shaped by our experiences as we deal with the unknown. It is what we do not know that we do not know that opens the door for great success.

I completed twenty-one miles today, and there was an overcast sky, which improved the walk tremendously. These were the first clouds I have seen since March 15! We attended a Mass celebration today at Saint Andrew the Apostle Church. I dedicated the prayers to the true heroes that I have met in my life. Those heroes understood the value of friendship, and for that, I am grateful. They understood the value of courage, both personal and moral courage, and understood the value of integrity and lived by it.

I also asked my Facebook friends to join with me in prayer for Janet Deal's dad and Bernadette Semple's brother-in-law.

March 31, 2014

Late yesterday, I heard that the brother-in-law of a dear friend of mine passed away unexpectedly. She asked me to remember her family in prayer. I found during my walk that asking for prayer gave comfort to those who asked. I probably should not have been surprised by that, but I was. Merely reaching out and touching someone in a personal way can have such tremendous impact on all of us. May he rest in peace, and may the family know that we were all praying for them. Try to reach out every day and call someone you have not talked in a long time and tell them that you miss them.

Life Lessons Learned: Friends matter, family matters, things do not.

This is the part of the walk of atonement that became so important to me. I asked the people whom I have hurt to forgive me, those that I have disappointed to pray for me, and those that I helped to help another.

The value of atonement is that it personalizes your accountability for what you have done and is so essential to the process of healing. We are forgiven by our Savior, but the healing comes when we atone.

Life Lessons Learned: Forgiveness comes from Christ, but atonement comes from within and completes the forgiveness.

Today is my brother Bob's birthday! I am extraordinarily fortunate to have Bob as my brother. He is a great brother, and I have nothing but fond memories of when we were growing up even though I still think Mom loves him more! At least that's what he told me every day. Happy birthday, brother Bob. I prayed for Bob at Mass today.

I think Bob took the death of our father in 1955 harder, because he knew Dad and saw the rawness of Dad's illness—lung cancer. I often said to Bob that I think that I was fortunate to be younger when Dad died, because I only had the memories of a three-year-old's impression of their hero, their dad. Bob, my brother Ed, and my sister Pat saw Dad and Mom during the very painful days preceding our dad's death. I prayed today that Bob would have the same youthful memories of our dad that I did.

I met Christi today at Corpus Christi Church. We had a very pleasant conversation and discussed how important it is to solve our society's problems in a compassionate way. I said that I was not sure how we were going to solve the problem of how to best financially support our children with emotional and behavioral issues, but I was hoping the walk and intervention by our Savior would give me the wisdom to understand how to do it.

During today's walk, two phenomenal things happened. First, I met a mom and her daughter and her daughter's caretaker as I was walking through Phoenix. We were talking about her daughter and the challenges that she has. I asked her mom if she believed in miracles, and she pointed to her daughter and said yes. It was one of the most gratifying and touching experiences in my life. This mom was an inspiration. I was delighted when she asked if we could have a picture taken together.

The second phenomenal thing occurred when I stopped by to see my good friends Jena and Mary and the staff at the Arizona Society of CPAs. I was so happy that they were aware of the trip from Bill Sheridan at the Maryland Association of CPAs and were so incredibly welcoming. I have lectured for Jenna and Mary many times in the past, and it was like a touch of home seeing them both.

The two experiences made for a great day all around.

On the mileage front, I have completed twenty miles so far today, and I'm seeing how my body's holding out to do more!

April 1, 2014

I completed seven miles this morning. Then I headed to Mass to say prayers for two friends being operated on today—Rosie and Cynthia. I told them both, "God will be with you today and every day."

I typically broke down each day of walking into four segments to eventually get back up to the adjusted mileage goal of twenty-five miles per day. What that allowed me to do was to get my nutrition balanced and to ensure that I rested along the way.

The nutrition and rest part of this journey surprised me more than I thought it would. Some of the challenges in the beginning of the walk were physical, such as gear and foot problems, but once those subsided, the impact of nutrition and rest came to the forefront.

Life Lessons Learned: **Rest and nutrition are critical to survival and thriving.**

I found that the advice that I received from Michele Wyman and Cynthia Lovewell, who are both nurses and medical professionals, was extraordinarily important. Michele reminded me to eat continuously from the time I started walking each day until I stopped. Cynthia reminded me to make sure that I used less sodium and to take more potassium. She had noticed in one of my pictures that my ankles and legs were experiencing some sort of reaction to excess sodium. Very astute observations on both persons' parts, and for that, I am thankful.

I was also surprised that by walking all the time and being sixty-two years old at that time that my joint flexibility was deteriorating by just walking and not doing other types of exercises to keep my muscles limber.

This was the point at which I decided to be much more careful about stretching and engaging in other types of flexibility exercises so that I could complete the journey. I truly did not expect that type of an issue to occur.

Life Lessons Learned: **Variety is the spice of life and is essential to well-being.**

During my early part of the walk, I was enjoying talking to my friend Ken Bancroft, with whom I worked at St. Agnes Hospital in Baltimore, Maryland. Ken is one of those friends for whom the word *gratitude* was designed, because I was so grateful to have him as a friend. We had many interesting days in the trenches during the transition of health care.

Having just talked with Ken, I received a note from another very close personal friend, Albert "Skip" Counselman, who was the chairman of the board of St. Agnes Hospital at the time Ken was president. Skip told me that Ken was going to have immediate cardiac surgery. I was stunned by the suddenness of what happened and how fragile life can be when I sent Skip this note:

> *Skip thank you for keeping me posted. Talked to Ken just a few days ago and he sent me a message this morning telling me what happened. What a shock but thank God it was diagnosed early. I will be definitely praying for him and I've also been praying for you and Margie and your family as well.*

Life Lessons Learned: **Life is short, time is precious, and friends are essential.**

Shortly after that summer note to Skip, it finally happened!

> *We are always taught in the Marines to always know your escape route and this time I seemed to forget that extremely valuable lesson. What happened was that someone started to follow me and as I noticed them following me I sped up to break free of the pursuer. The faster I seemed to go, admittedly not that fast, the faster he seemed to go. What happened next was I found myself in a corner with no way out except a small drain opening which violated every Marine Corps principle I had ever been taught. As I started to crawl through the drain opening he started to*

pull on my leg, just like I'm pulling on yours! :-). Happy
April Fools' day! :-)

I am so sorry about this (actually I am really not but it felt
like it was the right thing to say whether I meant it or not).
You know it just would not be me if I did not do this on
April Fools' Day.

Keeping a light note and a sense of humor was something that made
this trip bearable, particularly as I became more aware by the prayer
requests of how many people were experiencing trauma in their lives. It
was a wonderful time to reflect and pray.

Today I started to head out from Phoenix on my way to Payson, Arizona.
I expect to be in Payson area in about three days. I saw many miracles,
and we prayed for a miracle for my dear friend Ken tomorrow during
his surgery.

A good friend of mine suggested that it would be great to write a course
about the real meaning of life. One of the greatest things I am learning
is the value of slowing down and taking time to think. There is a
tremendous advantage to not be doing sixty miles per hour. It turns out
that when you sit down and engage with others near you, you will find
the world to be a more interesting and fun place to be. I have never been
so optimistic about a nation as I have been since meeting the wonderful
people that I have met thus far on this trip.

Life Lessons Learned: **Slow down, disconnect, clear your mind, and**
take time to think.

April 2, 2014

Today is my brother Ed's birthday! It was a great day to walk and pray.
I had another unbelievable day.

After doing fourteen miles, I stopped for a noon Mass at Saint Francis
Xavier Church in Phoenix to go to Mass for my brother Ed. The
reception that I received at the Jesuit church was nothing short of
miraculous. All the priests and everyone that worked there were so

hospitable and welcoming. What a true faith-based community. One person that I met, JoAnn, had such fond memories of Archbishop Lori when he was bishop of Bridgeport, Connecticut. Archbishop Lori is the archbishop of Baltimore, and he was so wonderful to write a nice letter of support for me for this walk. JoAnn wrote a letter to him and asked me to carry it back with me to give to him when I returned to Maryland, which I did.

Today a very dear friend of mine, Ken Bancroft, had open-heart surgery. I said a rosary for him and went to Mass for him as well.

My day was going great until I went to dinner. I was talking about the military to a few of the patrons and the owner of the restaurant. A number of us were former marines or retired marines as well as one service member from the navy. As I was getting ready to leave, one of the patrons stepped outside with me and asked if I had been in World War II or Korea. Apparently, this walk is making me look even worse than I thought I already did! Who says there is value to an ego! :)

On the way to Payson, I started climbing mountains again, and I noticed rain clouds. The clouds were a welcome relief from the sun even if I got wet. From the beginning of the walk on March 15 until now, there has been no rain. I came to welcome overcast skies from a personal perspective, but the local residents were hoping that those overcast skies would turn to rain due to the severe drought in that part of the United States.

Little did I know today that I would not see any rain for the first seventy-eight days of my trip!

Had there been extensive rain and had my feet gotten soaking wet, trench foot would become a major problem and potentially debilitating. Caring for one's feet was something we emphasized in the Marine Corps. I was incredibly fortunate and thankful to God every day that my feet could stay dry despite the discomfort.

My feet were literally decimated from the blisters.

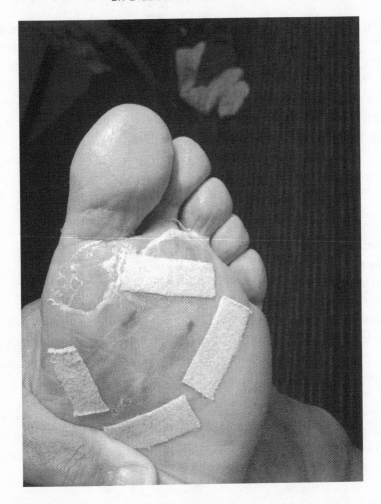

Life Lessons Learned: **Trials and tribulations may actually be blessings in disguise. We are not in control.**

A friend asked me how far I had gone.

> *Laura I've done about 395 miles so far. I wanted you know that I did pray for your family as you requested. Did you notice the pictures I sent for you?*

During the walk, many people would ask me how many miles I do each day. Today I wanted you to know that I completed twenty-two miles. This mileage count was also a great help for me because it allowed me to focus on getting my mileage back up to the revised target of twenty-five miles per day, which, if you recall, was well below the thirty-two miles per day that I had originally intended. This setback was just something I had to deal with. It was difficult at times to accept that I was not physically capable of doing the thirty-two miles per day that I originally intended due to some flaws that I had in my body and in my plan. But it was all good!

On a more important note, at Saint Francis Xavier Church, the staff and Father Sauer invited me for lunch after Mass.

During the discussion with Father Sauer, I was explaining what we do at Good Shepherd Services. He was so compassionate about our mission. And I am so proud of the sisters and our entire staff as well as our children.

In explaining why I was doing the walk without a support vehicle, I mentioned I was trying to experience what some of our children experience. There is a major difference though, and the difference is that I can quit at any time.

My walk is voluntary, but for our children, the behavioral, emotional, or developmental disabilities are not voluntary. That is the reason we have got to solve the problem of how to help our children. We must break the cycle and provide meaningful help.

April 3, 2014

Whoever does not believe in miracles, please give me a call. Through the intervention of your prayers, a dear friend of mine who had open-heart surgery is recovering nicely. That comes on top of the great results for Rosie and Cynthia.

We completed 24.2 miles, so the mileage is beginning to step up even though my feet are protesting loudly. The scenery and the hills on the way to Payson are absolutely breathtaking. Walking up hills is not particularly difficult. In fact, I actually welcome the climb in anticipation of what I can expect to see over the horizon. Going downhill is significantly more of a challenge, but I suspect a great deal of that has to do with the healing blisters and my age.

I just found out while walking about the tragedy at Fort Hood. Pray for those at Fort Hood that they may be able to handle the tragedy that has befallen them. I can only imagine what their families are going through with the dramatic change in their lives.

Life Lessons Learned: **Have empathy for one another. Caring is a most potent medicine.**

Diana Ellis posted this mileage update when we got to Mesa, Arizona: 361 miles down. All I kept thinking was that my feet were barely holding out and what would happen to the kids if I was not successful. I thought about what happened if I failed. I was convinced that failure was not going to be an option. Completing this journey would require faith and perseverance and the guiding hand of our Savior and the assistance of our Blessed Mother. I took comfort in knowing that I was not alone.

Life Lessons Learned: **With Christ on our side, failure is not an option.**

> April 3, 2014 - Day #20 - Mesa, AZ - 361 miles down, 2445 left to go! — with Frank Ryan

April 4, 2014

As I continued on the journey, I was mesmerized by the beauty of the mountains, the cactus, and the sheer isolation, peace, and tranquility of my surroundings.

I was surprised that the hills did not bother me or my feet. It dawned on me as I was walking that the awe of the moment distracted me from whatever discomfort I may have been feeling. I could not help but think of all that I have missed by driving sixty miles an hour on so many different highways throughout the world and only glancing at the beauty and tranquility around me.

As I was checking out the hills, the realization struck me that this was the tallest or steepest climbs I would be making in the next few days, and my mind kept going back to the journey from Poway to Julian, California. Then I started thinking about what happened when I went from Julian to Brawley. It just struck me that going from Payson, Arizona, up the Rim, as it is called and as I could see in the distance, put the pucker factor in me.

Life Lessons Learned: **Obstacles are nothing but tests of your drive, will, and faith.**

We completed 20.6 miles for the day and transitioned my equipment to Payson, Arizona. At one of the local restaurants, I met a wonderful family at dinner. They were so incredibly cordial and engaged me in conversation. They made me feel so welcome.

The scenery around Payson was so gorgeous. They call it the Rim Country, but I was not sure why. Stunning, absolutely stunning!

I also saw my first moose sign on the highway. I can only imagine what it will be like to be driving at seventy miles an hour and hit a moose. Thankfully, when walking at 2.5 miles an hour, it was not going to be an issue. Of course, I was going so slow there was a possibility a moose would start laughing at me! No kidding, I actually thought about that when I was walking. It just goes to show you what you think about when you have got an unbelievable amount of time on your hands. It was kind of nice.

April 5, 2014

I climbed one of the longest and steepest hills to get up to five thousand feet in Payson today. I have never traveled so high in such a short distance. Trust me though. Payson's beauty is worth it with both the beauty of the scenery and the kindness of its people.

We completed a little over twenty miles today. That hill kicked my butt! Pardon the expression! :-)

On Facebook, someone asked me how soon it would be before I got to Kansas and Indiana. It was an interesting question, because the realization that I had been going for twenty days and not yet gotten through two states was beginning to concern me. The question caused me to check the route and see when I would get through different states.

I am not sure why it was not a big deal with me before I started walking, but I had to put it in perspective. I realized then that California, Arizona, and New Mexico, just three states, are over one thousand miles of the 2,800-mile trip. Apparently, I am not going to be in Indiana or Kansas for a while!

I started laughing to myself as I began to wonder if it would be quicker to roll down some of these hills rather than try to walk down them. Seriously, walking down hills is more of a challenge than walking uphill. The stress on your ankles and knees is more than I thought. I ended up enjoying walking up hills because I enjoyed the challenge. On the downside, I loved seeing the scenery but was concerned about the physical strain on the body.

The question of how long it would take to get to Kansas and Indiana made me realize that I was behind schedule and it was going to be a very long time before I got to either state. I was also somewhat surprised that Indiana is farther east than I thought it was. I had a geography lesson with that one question.

I was honored to have the privilege of doing a Skype invocation for the Pennsylvania Leadership Conference. It was arranged by my dear friend Lowman Henry, who is the president of the Lincoln Institute. It was a wonderful opportunity to connect with friends. It was just interesting to know that we were sharing the issue of the needs of our children with so many great people. Lowman, thank you so much!

The invocation reminded me that this is all about the children.

I received a very nice Facebook message from Father Bill Kuchinsky. Father Bill is the chaplain for this walk and a very dear friend. I met Father Bill on a pilgrimage to Lourdes, France. I am honored to call him my friend. He was teasing me a little about my comments about my feet and blisters, and I told them that I was going to rename the walk as the "Limp across America."

I said that somewhat tongue-in-cheek comment about limping and about the blisters, but one of the things that this walk have finally taught me is that I have so much to be thankful for. I said in the past this was a walk of gratitude, but I think Father Bill's question and joking convinced me to stop being concerned about minor inconveniences. Sometimes it is important as a friend to help keep us grounded. Compared to what so many millions of people go through, I have it pretty easy, and I hope to always be grateful and share the wonderful gifts I have been given with others. I would learn in Kansas the wonderful expression "Pay it forward."

Life Lessons Learned: A true friend tells you what you need to hear, not what you want to hear.

April 6, 2017

Today I received one of the most magnificent messages I could ever possibly hope for. Ken Bancroft, who had open-heart surgery this week, sent me an audio recording wishing us well on our mission. He is my hero.

I had the chance to work with Ken and saw him deal with integrity, grace, and humility at a time when it would have been easy to do something other. I prayed for him since his surgery and will continue to do so. The world is a better place because of him.

As I walk, I would find coins along the road and would pick them up to be able to donate to Good Shepherd. I like to design medallions, and we did design a medallion for our mission and the Sisters of the Good Shepherd.

As a result, whenever I found a coin on the road, it reminded me of the beliefs of the sisters, which is that regardless of the child, that child always has value. On our medallion, it says that our mission is to care for the most abandoned soul. The Sisters of the Good Shepherd always remind me that we have to take care of one child at a time. That comment reinforced the idea that everyone has value. Some of the coins that I found were pretty damaged, but they still had value.

At the end of the day, our relationship with our Savior and the friends we have and the people we have impacted is what is most important.

Life Lessons Learned: **Care for the most abandoned soul. Everyone has value.**

April 7, 2014

Today was another one of those days where a sense of humor was needed. I was frequently getting stopped by well-wishers, caring police, and others offering me assistance. Invariably, someone would ask me what I was doing, and I would say that I was walking across America, or limping across America, as the case may be, and they thought that I was going from east to west. Many of them, when they saw me walking east, assumed that I got turned around and was heading the wrong way. When I told them that I was walking from the West Coast to the East Coast and with the realization came that I was still in the infancy of the walk, you could see the anguish in their face, particularly since they knew I was going to have to walk up the Rim in the next day. It was touching and funny at the same time.

At Mass in Payson, Arizona, I met Father Edward Lucero. What an absolutely wonderful person. He was so accommodating and spiritual that it warmed my heart. At Mass, when I was telling him my plan for the next day, he cautioned me about the Rim, and he said that by the time I left Payson and got to the Rim, it would be toward the end of day and I would probably be too exhausted to reach the summit. He advised me to do most of the walk to the base of the Rim, stop for the evening, and then climb the Rim when I am fresh in the morning the following day.

I took his advice, and it was incredibly helpful. Had I tried to climb the Rim at the end of the day, I would have had some difficulties.

The experience pointed out some interesting issues for me.

First, how do you know which advice to take and which advice to ignore?

Life Lessons Learned: **Be willing to listen.** *Listen* **has the same letters as** *silent*. **Seldom do you learn by talking.**

Second, I was stunned that with all my advanced planning, I never thought of getting a contour map of the area. I know better than that from my days in the Marine Corps, and the lack of foresight on my part on this critical matter stunned me.

This helped explain to me how I was shaped by my experiences. I spent most of my life on the East Coast. We typically do not have hills like those in Payson near me, although we do have steep terrain in the Appalachians. That being said, I looked at my surroundings in the East Coast and did not anticipate what I was going to run into at the Rim in Payson. As my younger friends would say, "My bad."

The other issue is, how do you know when to take advice and when not to? Just as I am shaped by my experiences, so are other people. I had people who were so apprehensive about what I was doing that they encouraged me to stay away from certain areas because of their fears. Their fears are shaped by their experiences, although they can also be shaped by sound judgment. The challenge is to know which is which. I became convinced and remain so to this day that it was because of the hand of God that the right decisions were made. It was no accident. I firmly believe that I am protected by our Savior and his mother.

Life Lessons Learned: **Judgment and logical thinking are critical. Teach our children how to think, not what to think.**

April 8, 2014

The day for climbing the Rim has begun. I received a wonderful wakeup call this morning.

> *Good morning brother! Father Bill sent me a Reveille call this morning and I loved it!*

Well, after much climbing, we made it!

Through the power of prayer, we made it to the top of the rim! The exhilaration at reaching the summit brought tears to my eyes. I have never seen such beauty! I was giddy.

The majesty, the tranquility, and the sheer scope of the scenery reminded me of the love of the Most Holy Trinity and the mother of Jesus has for all of us. I started to think of all those who allowed me the time to make this trip.

My son Matt and I started working together two months before I left for this journey. I was thinking of how hard that must have been for him to take over after such a short period. I am so proud of him and all my children.

I was also thinking of the challenge that Sherrie had as she balanced the house, her own work schedule, the dogs, and also helping take care of her father, who was very ill. John Costa, Sherrie's dad, was a retired navy chief and was suffering from a recently diagnosed mesothelioma. We had considered canceling the walk because of so much uncertainty. He held on and fought the valiant battle when he finally returned home to God on May 23, 2014.

I felt somewhat selfish seeing this beauty while others were working so hard to support what we were trying to do for our children. I prayed that I would never take this trip for granted.

As I was reaching the top, my friend Karl Ahlrichs sent me a note wishing me well and asking me to give him an estimate of how the altitude was. I responded to him by saying, "Karl my attitude holding up just nicely! Oh, oh, oh, you said altitude! I'm at about 7800 feet for most of those pictures. Now I'm at a little bit over 8000 feet."

Some other comments that I received included one from Ken Bancroft, who was still recovering from surgery. I said to him, "Ken great to hear from you! Blessed Mother, Our Savior, and all of my friends came with me. The person in the picture was the wife of a couple that agreed to take my picture at the top of the hill as I was ordered to by Diana Ellis!"

Once I climbed the Rim, I was in the high desert. It was as dry as the lower desert areas, but the temperature was comfortable and in the seventies.

The logistics needed for this journey became apparent when I got to the Rim and the temperature dropped suddenly. This was the point at which I realized that I needed to make certain that I double-checked weather forecasts each day before I started walking. Prior to today, I did not have to worry about that because the temperature was consistently hot. Now, though, it was likely to be cool in the morning, warm by midday, and extremely hot by late afternoon. Each of those circumstances require different.

We completed twenty miles. Last night I was fairly convinced that my feet would not sustain the climb due to the bruises and blisters. I prayed about it and just asked for guidance and direction from our Savior, the Holy Spirit, and the Blessed Mother. This morning, I woke up with no pain in my feet, feeling like a million bucks, and the climb went incredibly well because I actually had nothing to do with it! You cannot convince me of anything other than that! Your prayers did it. Thank you so much.

Life Lessons Learned: **When in doubt, pray. Actually, pray all the time!**

April 9, 2014

While walking, I carried a list of people for whom I was going to be praying that day. I began the list with people who asked for prayers before I started walking and always added people to pray for as I met them along my route. I would always pray the rosary as well as a group of prayers for each person I was praying for. Finally, there were a series of prayers of Hail Mary prayers, Our Fathers, and Glory Be to the Father. It gave me a chance to reflect on each person. I genuinely enjoyed having the time to pray.

As I walked, I would also hear of different world events and would add those victims to my prayer request. Today I heard the news report of the students who had been harmed in Murrysville, Pennsylvania. I asked all those that were following my walk,

> *Please pray for the students have been injured in Murrysville PA. Please protect them and their families from any further harm. Emotional and behavioral health is so critically important for all let alone young children.*

It is amazing the wonderful people you meet when you slow down and "smell the roses." My walking speed has set a new definition for the word *slow*!

The day started in Holbrook, Arizona. I parked my support vehicle at the Navajo County administrative buildings and asked for permission to leave my car in the parking lot while I walked back across the high desert. On the way out of the admin building, I met a woman who was struggling with some books going into the courthouse. I asked her if I could help her. She was very thankful for the assistance and proceeded to tell me, after I told her about Good Shepherd, that she had adopted a sixteen-year-old girl who had some of the same life experiences as some of our children at Good Shepherd.

The road was incredibly flat for the twenty miles I did today compared to what I have been experiencing for the first twenty-five days of the trip. A great time to reflect without too much physical exertion!

One of the things I noticed while I was walking was the smells. The trees in the forest had the aroma of a Christmas tree. The pine tree smell was so peaceful that I stopped for a few minutes to soak up the beautiful aromas. It was like an entire forest of Christmas trees. It reminded me so much of family time during the holidays.

I had a late dinner today, and at the restaurant, I had the opportunity to meet two young people, Sarah and Natalie. Sarah's moving back to the States, and they agreed to have their picture taken with me. They were so wonderful to put up with the ramblings of an old person at dinner.

April 10, 2014

> Thursday, April 10th - Day #27 - Holbrook, AZ -
> 508 miles down, 2298 left to go. 18.1% of the route
> completed! — with Frank Ryan.

The scenery was remarkable. I was overwhelmed by the diversity and immensity of our nation. For some reason, in all the times that I had driven cross-country, I never had the same perspective.

That change in perspective is often a form of empathy for others as well. Can you imagine yourself in someone else's position? If you were to switch places, what would you want?

It is interesting that the walk has been teaching me a great deal about patience. I was at dinner and talking about the mission of Good Shepherd Services with two people who were from Denver. They were heading to Phoenix, and I mentioned that should only take two hours or slightly more. That same distance for me was pretty close to seven days.

Life Lessons Learned: **Be patient. All good things come in time.**

April 11, 2014

One of the additional lessons that I am learning during this trip, in addition to patience, is persistence. You have to want to do this walk to get it done. In a similar but much more important fashion, the Sisters of the Good Shepherd are persistent in their drive to take care of the most abandoned soul, all in the name of the Savior and humanity and for the benefit of children.

As I see the homelessness and drifters as I travel across the United States, I cannot help but wonder how many of these wonderful people were adversely affected as children where prompt intervention might have had a huge impact in their lives. Persistence!

Consistency, judgment, compassion, respect, and love are all part of the plan we need to help one another. I met those five principles today in a Denny's restaurant in Holbrook, Arizona. It was colder out than I expected when I was walking, so I stopped to get a cup of coffee to go.

Life Lessons Learned: **Consistent, judgment, compassion, respect, and love solve problems.**

Shelley, who got me some coffee, and the store manager were incredibly hospitable. The store manager introduced me to about five or six other patrons and let me talk about our mission.

The respect and compassion that I felt from them reminded me that that is what our mission is all about.

I have learned a great deal on this trip. The spiritual awakening has been profound. I think I am beginning to get a PhD. But it's not the PhD that you may think.

It is a PhD of philosophy, helpfulness, and direction.

Two of the biggest creature comforts that I have missed during the past month are something that you will find to be absolutely silly: coffee and a place to sit.

I took them for granted.

When I do work for those in need, I interpret their needs based upon my experiences, not theirs. I cloak my help in my own experiences and perceptions.

I am beginning to realize that many times, my help may have actually been worthless to them. It was what I thought that they needed and not what they actually needed.

I often wonder whether I listened through my ears or theirs. Did I listen to understand?

I am beginning to wonder whether or not that is the real problem. Are we attempting to solve problems based upon our own experiences or the experiences of those we need to help?

Perhaps listening to people is the greatest PhD we can ever get.

Life Lessons Learned: **Take nothing for granted.**

A friend of mine and fellow instructor, Jennifer Elder, asked me about my impressions so far:

> *Jennifer I could not agree with you more. Absolutely believe that I always interpreted people's needs based upon what they needed but now I know that I did not. After 27 days of walking in the sun, I now understand why people who are indigent sleep under bridges. It's cooler by about 20° and provides protection from the elements. The bench is just a nice ability to relax. It's so much more comfortable to sit on the bench than on the ground. Your comments are extremely wise!*

We completed a little over twenty miles today. I am on the way to Albuquerque to move my base of operations from Holbrook, Arizona, to Albuquerque, New Mexico, and to stage the equipment for the next leg of the journey. Having the support vehicle is so helpful in that the logistics effort before that was consuming so much of the walking day that I was concerned that it would delay the journey by many months if we did not resolve it made the journey possible, but the process did take a while to get used to.

April 12, 2014

I got in to Albuquerque late last evening. I decided to do my walking in Albuquerque and then on Monday of this coming week to start backtracking the areas that I skipped over.

I saw polar opposites today that just intrigued me. The implications of it are profound in my mind.

When I first started walking, I saw a group of hot air balloons and envisioned the positive experiences that all the riders were having.

At the end of my walk, I saw an etching in the sidewalk that said "Trust no one." I thought of how sad it must be to have lost hope such that you cannot trust anyone.

That is precisely what many children experience and deal with. They have lost hope.

Life Lessons Learned: One of the greatest gifts to give is hope. Christ is hope.

We have to do whatever we can to give these children that hope and trust again so that they can start to experience the life that Christ had in store for them.

Whenever you are working with children with emotional and behavioral issues, I encourage you to remember that it is not only what you do for the children but also what you promised to do to help that matter.

My hair was getting a little shaggy after almost twenty-eight days without a haircut. For a marine, that's like an eternity! I had to get a haircut. I went to Theo's family barbershop in Albuquerque and had a chance to spread the message about our children.

We completed twenty-one miles today. I truly did not think I was going to get more than three or four miles because I only got one hour of sleep last night. It was one of those rare nights where I was so tired that I could not sleep peacefully.

On Monday I go back and retrace the steps that I jumped over when I came out of Holbrook, Arizona.

The distances are so great between Holbrook and Albuquerque that I am using Albuquerque as a base of support for about fifteen days. I will be staging unneeded gear there so that I can navigate the altitudes and the desert more easily. I was surprised that operating at between 6,000 and 7,500 feet was not what I expected. I slowed down speed-wise but never felt any oxygen deprivation.

I also must tell you that since I started walking, I have yet to run into anyone who has not been supportive of what Good Shepherd Services is doing. The response has been so heartwarming. This was the first time that it was obvious to me that everyone has been so kind and compassionate. I started to realize today that my cynicism was starting to go away. What a great feeling.

Life Lessons Learned: Cynicism is a thief. It steals your energy. It robs your heart.

April 13, 2014

I spent a very peaceful Palm Sunday at Saint Charles Church in Albuquerque, New Mexico.

I posted on Facebook:

> *Happy Palm Sunday!*
> *You are all in my thoughts and prayers.*
> *For my family, I miss you and I love you.*

First, I went to a wonderful Mass on Palm Sunday. After that, at 3:00 PM PDT, I had the opportunity to meet with a number of candidates for the third degree for the Knights of Columbus in Albuquerque at Saint Charles Church.

Will Buttarazzi; the state director of the Knights of Columbus for New Mexico, Peter; and the grand knight Anthony were so supportive. I received a very warm reception when I talked about our mission and our plans at Good Shepherd. Albuquerque was experiencing the effects of what happens when childhood behavioral issues are not dealt with.

The challenges of the homeless in the city were palpable. Homelessness was an epidemic. The scene of so many homeless and the chance to talk with many of them made me appreciate that this walk is about solving the problem for children to reduce the likelihood of homelessness and emotional and behavioral problems later in life.

On the hiking front, I noticed the winds for the first time! I had no idea that this was just the beginning of a month-long odyssey of winds and temperature that would prove to be a delightful but unexpected challenge.

I had a fantastic dinner at Rudy's. Unbelievable brisket and cream corn!

When I was walking, I ran into a Happy Feet store. I almost convinced myself that the store was opened because of me.

April 14, 2014

When I left the East Coast to go on this journey, the temperatures were consistently well below thirty degrees. In fact, in late February of 2014, I was in Bozeman, Montana, and it was thirty degrees below zero.

For much of the trip in California, I had been in ninety-degree weather but was getting weather report from home that it was still snowing even in April. When I went into the high desert, the temperatures dropped drastically, so I told my friends on Facebook,

> For all my East Coast friends that have been lamenting the fact that I've been in 90° weather for most of this trip, rest assured I'm wearing winter clothing today and it snowed just east of where I am right now! Was beginning to think I would not need my winter clothes! :-)

Since it was Easter week, I decided to go to Mass every day. Easter Week is such a great time of reflection for me as a Catholic.

One of the disadvantages of walking is that you lose track of time. I completely forgot that today was Monday. I went to go to Mass at 7:00 AM but forgot that today was Monday and there was no Mass at the church I was going to. It was a wonderful walk anyway. ☺

I learned two things today. First is the importance of preplanning as much as you can, and the second is embracing the unexpected. When you walk an hour or more and then find out it was for naught, it can get a little frustrating.

Life Lessons Learned: **Embrace the unexpected.**

I am sure you have felt one of those frustrating days in which you worked very hard but accomplished nothing. That happens. The challenge is to not let that setback affect you. When walking, the time-distance metric changes drastically compared to what you are used, and thus, embracing the unexpected becomes incredibly important. You can either look at it with grace and dignity or look at it with frustration. The decision is yours.

This is not to say I did not get frustrated, but I was mentally trying to make sure that I always tried to take a positive approach on what was happening. By this point, I realized the walk was more of a mental challenge than a physical one.

As I was continuing my trek in New Mexico, I came across the New Mexico Society of CPA offices. I stopped by and got a wonderfully warm reception from all my friends at the New Mexico Society of CPAs.

As with Arizona and California, I have to admit that all the folks that I have met so far have been absolutely phenomenal.

We had good walking distances for the past two days. We ended up with seventeen miles yesterday and 21.5 miles today! I always needed to remind myself that I could have driven that distance in forty-five minutes, but then I think I would have missed the point.

As I walked, I got to know a few of the homeless people in Albuquerque.

A homeless person that I saw today seemed a little distraught when he saw the Albuquerque Police Department. I was standing near him, and he was clearly apprehensive. The police relations with the homeless had been a hot topic nationally for a while.

The police, though, were very kind and considerate. The homeless person was also trying to be very nice but was obviously scared. Nothing happened except that it was clear to me that a society that fails to deal with behavioral and emotional issues with children will have to deal with the same issues when those children become adults.

Life Lessons Learned: **Deal with reality. Reality only changes when we face adversity head-on.**

The meaning of life becomes apparent when walking.

As a CPA, I often wish that we could construct the study that would show the real impact of failure to develop serious solutions to serious problems. *Life Lessons Learned*: **Trust is the foundation of any great relationship.**

April 15, 2014

I was having breakfast at Little Anita's in Albuquerque after walking to church and before heading up to Chimayo for the religious ceremonies, when I ran into David Buehler and a friend of his, both of whom are air force ROTC cadets.

I was extraordinarily impressed with them. Our nation is in great hands with the leaders like this! I know a number of air force generals who are friends, and I am going to make sure they are aware that they are selecting some pretty fine officers!

Another lesson in my walk is that we have fine young people in our nation, and we are in good hands. I work with one of my sons and am extremely proud of him and all my children. The role of mentoring children so that they can make their greatest contribution to society is one of the major issues facing parents and our nation.

As with what I found with people in general when I am walking, people and young people in particular are pretty decent human beings. We cannot let the constant negativity that sells news cloud our judgment about which really is going on. I did not know it yet, but when I got to Highland, Illinois, this thought would be reinforced when I met a wonderful retired marine by the name of Bill Napper who started a newspaper that only prints good news.

As happened on Monday, I was heading to church and found out that the church services had changed a little during Easter week.

Despite the change, our Savior allowed me to meet a number of wonderful people today that made the entire day and trip worthwhile. Embracing the unexpected!

The first was Barbara Zachary at Saint Charles Church in Albuquerque. She has been with the church for thirty-four years and was incredibly hospitable to me in showing me different areas where I could worship this week. When I asked her if I might pray for her or her friends, she immediately gave me the names of people other than herself. You can see the love in her eyes for her children, grandchildren, friends, and her faith.

At breakfast at Little Annie's, where I met the two AFROTC cadets, I also met Angie, a young woman who had five grandchildren she adored. She was telling me about her two-year-old granddaughter, Nicolette, who was having medical issues. You could see Angie's love for her family. As we continued to talk, she told me that her goals in life was to set up two not-for-profits, one to help abandoned children and one that would help elderly people. I was so proud of her, and I knew she would accomplish her goals.

Due to the Holy Week festivities, I decided to do part of the walk with the pilgrimage to Chimayo.

What a beautiful pilgrimage! What a wonderful time of year to visit such a holy site.

Chimayo is a very holy site in New Mexico. Virtually, everyone in New Mexico is aware of it, and everyone that I met was so willing to assist me in getting there to experience this wonderful Holy Week tradition.

Many of the highways that I could have walked were not authorized for pedestrian traffic. During this journey, that caused me to divert occasionally. During this Holy Week, though, the major interstate going from Albuquerque to Chimayo was open for pedestrian traffic. I saw people of all ages making this pilgrimage. Some were carrying crosses for the entire journey. It was awe-inspiring and breathtaking as well as very humbling.

We completed 23.9 miles, and my feet and stamina are feeling much better even though I climbed some pretty steep hills. Your prayers are working!

I never cease to be amazed at the genuine kindness of so many people regardless of their stage in life.

I was in Chimayo and met Paulette and Brian, and they were incredibly considerate and generous with their time in explaining the history of the area.

Also, at the end of the day, I was doing my laundry. One of the folks in the Laundromat had some additional time left on his machine and was more than considerate enough to share that time with others. It seems like a small detail, but it is an act of consideration that we should never forget the significance of.

Random acts of kindness are everywhere. We just have to look for them.

Life Lessons Learned: **Practice random acts of kindness. It will be the greatest gift you give to yourself.**

April 16, 2014

Today I was walking along the Rio Grande. The scenery was breathtaking. It gave me time to reflect on some wonderful memories.

On this day in 1993, my mom passed away. It was a turning point in my life relative to my faith. I have always believed, but the power of miracles became apparent to me that day.

That miraculous part of that day in 1993 started with me having lunch in Baltimore. No big deal. But then I had an urging to call my mom at noon. What was unusual was that I *never* called my mom during the day. I always talked to her in the evening. We were both night owls.

For some reason, which I believe to be divine intervention, I called my mom at 1:00 PM.

A gentleman at the assisted-living facility answered my mom's phone and asked if I was a member of the family. I said that I was, and he suggested that I get to Frederick Maryland immediately.

I drove there as fast as I could. When I got there, my mom was near death. While I was praying with my mom, I looked out the window and noticed my sister Pat and my sister Gene. They had the same strange desire to come see my mom that day as well.

So with that intervention, my mom was able to pass with three of her five children by her side.

The peace in her eyes knowing that all her children on earth and all our spiritual family in heaven loved her was the most tranquil and peaceful feeling I have known in my life.

Weeks later, as we were sorting through Mom's effects, we found a love letter that she had written to my dad *after* he had died. She told him how we all missed him, but she knew that we would all be together again soon.

This morning at breakfast, I had French toast. It was the first time since my mom used to make French toast for us that I tasted something just like she made. What a wonderful memory of a great woman.

If your parents are still alive, put this book down now and give them a call and tell them that you love them.

If they have passed, say a prayer to them. They will hear you.

Life Lessons Learned: **Parents, love your children. Children, love your parents.**

We completed a little over twenty-two miles on the Rio Grande today. The beauty of the river cascading through Albuquerque is without parallel.

The Rio Grande is the lifeblood of the city and candidly of a good bit of the state.

I was struck by the number of beavers and how many trees were taken down by those little guys. They give you a different perspective on the word *persistence*!

April 17, 2014

When I woke up this morning, I was greeted with this post on Facebook.:

> *The April edition of The Statement is available online,*
> *with Frank Ryan's* Walk Across America *on the cover.*

This article had an interesting impact on me. It reinforced how considerate everyone at the Maryland Association of CPAs was to me, particularly Tom Hood, Pam Devine, Chris Doherty, Donna Carson, Emily Trout, Laura Shaner-Dorsey, and the entire MACPA team. But it also convinced me that I cannot quit. Literally, the pucker factor hit me when I realized how much I would be letting the children down if I quit.

I would find out in just a few days that that decision point would come and I would have to deal with possibly quitting. I believe in God! I believe that he allowed that article to come out when it did to give me the strength I would need to overcome the obstacle that I would face.

From my good friend Alexis Hyyppa: What a great article!

We got twenty-four miles in today! I am feeling great. I am getting feeling back in my toes. The blisters have become one continuous blister, but they are turning into a nice-looking foot ornament!

Today I met a number of great students from the University of New Mexico.

What a wonderful attitude, wonderful spirit, and wonderful drive. The staff at the Village Inn, where we had lunch, to include Crystal, Kerry, and Chasidy, was extremely helpful as well. It was just one of those high points where people interacting with one another made the day so special.

The walk was a spiritual one as well. The last one mile took almost two hours, but it was in a procession for Holy Thursday. Best walk of my life.

With the Holy Week, I remembered my family and all my friends that I was away from!

April 18, 2014—Good Friday

On Good Friday, I made my pilgrimage to Tome Hill in New Mexico, south of Albuquerque.

The legions of the faithful making this pilgrimage on this Good Friday were heartwarming.

> *May you all have a very holy and blessed Good Friday. Our Savior died for our salvation.*

The climb to the top of Tome Hill was physically challenging because of the rocks and the uneven surfaces. None of that mattered though, because I was with so many people who were going for the same reason, and that was to worship together on this Good Friday.

> *What a wonderfully spiritual day!*
> *You were all in my prayers.*
> *Absolutely beautiful area and wonderful people.*

April 19, 2014

I climbed Boca Negra Canyon walls today. Wow, wow, wow!

Whose idea was this anyway!?! ☺

I began to realize that I use that expression every time I overcame an obstacle and was exhilarated by the success. These moments of exhilaration become important as intermediate goals to accomplishing the ultimate objective.

Life Lessons Learned: **When the goal is far away, set intermediate goals.**

When there is a very long-term project, setting intermediate goals is essential so that it gives you another benchmark prior to continuing the journey. It helps with your morale to set intermediate goals.

As I was traveling across the United States, I could not help but remember those servicemen and women who are away from their families on the holidays.

> *As you celebrate this Easter with your family please say a prayer for all of those servicemen and women who are separated from their families because of their deployments.*
>
> *We are able to live free because of their sacrifices.*
>
> *Semper Fi and happy Easter!*

Had a wonderful day today, and the rain did not start until after I was finished. This was the first rain I have seen since March 15, but it was only a drizzle and lasted only minutes. I did not even get wet.

I spent a great deal of time today walking along Route 40 as well as seeing some of the extinct volcanoes right off Route 40.

I had time to think about the best solutions to help people with behavioral or emotional issues and/or developmental disabilities. The solutions were not yet apparent, but I was able to spend the time I needed to frame the problem and examine current efforts and their strengths and weaknesses, while we attempt to develop an overall approach to how we can best and consistently help one child at a time.

The value of each child's life cannot be underestimated.

The tranquility of the scenery is giving me a great time to think. I am beginning to understand why our Savior went to the desert to pray. The solitude is very helpful to clear the mind and focus. You should try it sometime.

I went to Mass this evening with Father Jerry for the Easter services, and it was tremendous. He is such an outstanding priest and spiritual educator. The way Father Jerry discussed Easter week put a meaning in it that I had not yet thought about. Thought-provoking and spiritual.

I received many wonderful messages wishing me a happy Easter.

Those kind messages had a bigger impact on me than I thought they would. It meant that someone cared enough to take time to say hello. Imagine the impact we could have been to so many people if we did that same thing. Try it. You will like it.

April 20, 2014

Happy Easter was all I could think about. I was at Saint Charles Church in Albuquerque for Easter services.

What a blessed day!

I had planned on taking a relatively easy day because it was Easter and because it was Sunday. I did not view the walk as work since it is a prayer walk, but I did want to soak up the solemnity of the day.

I was walking in Petroglyph National Park. Then it happened. I was not sure what it was, but I felt my ankle snap. It was not a break-type snap. It was more of a ligament or muscle pop that I have never experienced before. I went down.

As I think about it, it did not hurt tremendously, but it was more uncomfortable. I wrote on Facebook:

> *Well I think I finally did it. I was hiking and something snapped in my ankle so I'm going to ask you for your prayers as I get this thing checked out right now.*
>
> *Miss you guys.*

I received an unbelievable number of messages on Facebook. They meant a great deal.

> *Patsy thank you for your thoughts. I've made a commitment to these children and I'm going to complete (the walk) no matter what. It just may take me longer than I expected.:)*

Thank you all for your prayers. The urgent care department is closed on Sundays so I hope to have this thing checked out early Monday morning. I'm pretty certain it's not the Achilles' heel because it's not excruciatingly painful.

Just so that everyone is aware, the only impact this will have on the walk is that I may finish it on crutches or be on crutches for a few days.

As we look at this Easter season, we must remember that our Savior was crucified for us, so my ankle, like the blisters, is a mild inconvenience.

Right about at this point, the article that the MACPA published only three days earlier hit me like a brick. I made up my mind that these children and our mission were much more important than my ankle. I was not sure how I was going to make the walk, but I was going to make it. I kept thinking of the bravado of my earlier comment of doing it on crutches and thought to myself that I was an idiot.

I had to learn to embrace the unexpected again and pray for a solution, because the walk must be completed. Just limping on crutches was but one potential solution. I realized that there was much medical uncertainty, so I had to be patient to let it just play out. It was not in my hands.

Then it hit me. That is exactly what most people in society, including me, do with our children with emotional, behavioral, and developmental disabilities. Are we crafting solutions to problems we do not understand?

This little incident with the ankle convinced me that the solution that we need to come up with is a process and not an end state. We have to create a system that is faith based and always values the child. We need to develop an intellectual process and a spiritual process to be able to change the way we deal with our children as circumstances of society change.

In other words, developing a fixed solution rather than a dynamic process would have been a mistake. All this came from an ankle injury.

Life Lessons Learned: **Learning never ends. Change is the status quo.**

God works in mysterious ways. You may never know why you are going through such discomfort, but he has a plan for us all, so accept it.

By the way, I got five miles done today before this all happened.

The drawings from ancient times were beautiful. Can you guess which one of the petroglyphs said "Watch where you're walking"? :-)

April 21, 2014

I received this wonderful message from my dear friend Sr. Mary Catherine of the Sisters of the Good Shepherd. As with many of the sisters that I have met in my life, their selfless devotion to others humbles me.

> *Dear Frank, I hold you in prayer. We look forward to seeing you when you reach St. Louis. Sr. M. Catherine— in Saint Louis, Missouri.*

I went to the University of New Mexico Hospital this morning, and I waited for x-rays. I was stunned by the compassion and care that I received. I was in the clinic because this was not an emergency. I noticed the staff dealt compassionately with everyone. God bless them.

The medical report came in. I got great news—great news in every respect.

First, the best news of all was that I had the chance to meet some of the most compassionate, caring, dedicated health-care professionals that I have seen in a long time. The staff at the University of New Mexico medical facility was outstanding.

Second, they fitted me with a leg brace, and I was good to keep walking after I take a twenty-four-hour stand-down.

I am on the road again!
The prayers that I received from all of you were tremendous.

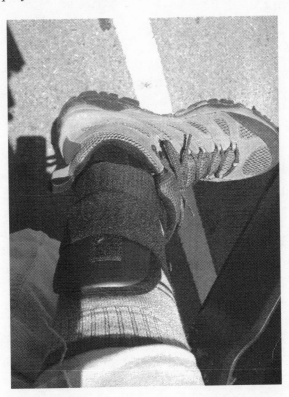

I wanted to test the leg brace to see how it may rub on my foot with my boots. I was happy with the results and was able to do about 6.5 miles with the brace with no significant challenges.

I am going to try to do at least fifteen miles tomorrow in Grants, New Mexico, over the Continental Divide.

Grants is west of Albuquerque, but I bypassed initially so I could establish my base of support in Albuquerque.

I need to make up about forty-two miles in the Grants area before I head to Santa Rosa.

After the Continental Divide, I only have one more major mountain to cross before I head into the Plains of the United States. After that one mountain east of Albuquerque, New Mexico, it is all downhill for just another 1,500 miles or until I run into the Appalachian Mountains.

April 22, 2014

The day is going great!

First, I had breakfast with some friends from Grants, New Mexico. The reception that they have given me was nothing short of extraordinary. Chris, his entire family, and the Knights of Columbus in Grants, New Mexico, made me feel like I was part of the family.

I saw in many parts of New Mexico the impact of when government and businesses do not work well together in the past and the impact that it has on current generations and their families. For instance, the mining and nuclear industries in New Mexico suffered substantial setbacks due to environmental and nuclear concerns. While that affected the business, obviously, as well as the local government, the impact on the individuals and families was catastrophic.

I think that what I saw most here was an area devastated by changes in their lives, but their faith and love of their families got them through. As I met with Chris and his family and saw so many other people here,

I realized that they have their priorities straight. In times of adversity, your faith and your family and your friends will see you through.

Life Lessons Learned: **In times of adversity, your faith and your family will see you through. You are not alone.**

In my case, during this walk, Greg Conderacci, Karl Ahlrichs, Pam Divine, and Diana Ellis, as well as so many other friends and family were my support group. In reality, with me on this walk were our Savior and his mother. It gave me a warm feeling inside to know that while I might seem to be isolated, I was really in the best of company and enjoying every moment of it.

Second, I crossed the Continental Divide, and I have got to tell you, the scenery is superior!

I was able to complete an update from Blue Ocean Ideas today. I enjoyed hearing from Brian. He was a delight to talk with, and since we were on Skype, it allowed me to see a face with the words. Thank you, Brian. You made the trip even more worthwhile.

Frank updates us from New Mexico . . . thank you MACPA and Blue Ocean Ideas for sharing.

MACPA member and Business Learning Institute *instructor* Frank Ryan *is walking coast to coast to raise awareness for Good Shepherd Services. To learn more visit* http://followfrank.macpa.org/

In the midst of walking through New Mexico Frank stops to bring us up to date on his Walk Across America.

We completed 20.5 miles for the first time with my new leg brace. I found that it slowed me down a little, but at least I can keep walking! It turns out that having arthritis in my ankle with bone spurs is what created the problem with the "snap" that I felt, so I just have to be careful not to twist it or do anything abnormal. Is walking 2,806 miles abnormal? :-)

April 23, 2014

April 23, 2014 - Day #40 - Albuquerque, NM - 762 miles down, 2044 left to go! 27% of the walk completed!

Message from Ryan Wey: "Go Frank go, you're almost out of the Midwest!!"

In the sorrowful mysteries of the rosary, which I prayed today, there is a phrase that I find so particularly helpful and has such huge impact in how we can help our children.

My children, pray to the Father that he will heal the wounds of your heart so that you can pray with love.

The children we care for have many issues that they need to be able to resolve, and with Christ's love, such healing is possible. That is why our mission is to care for the most abandoned soul—one child at a time!

The winds were strong today. I now realized that weather was going to play a critical element for the remainder of the trip. I had that perspective earlier in the journey, but it became very apparent today. Despite the winds, the challenge of dealing with it became a game and something that I looked forward to. I think, for the first time, I realized that I was enjoying the unknown.

Life Lessons Learned: Obstacles overcome become the adrenaline of life.

I have had many people ask me for guidance on what they should do to prepare to walk across the United States or to walk across America. I would think the greatest preparation you can do is to learn to embrace the unexpected.

For example, if I had started walking at a different time of the year, the weather in the various parts of the country would have been different. So if someone reads this journal and says be careful about heavy winds in eastern Arizona, New Mexico, Texas, Oklahoma, and Kansas, they may be woefully unprepared if they left at a different time of year.

Embracing the unexpected and being able to deal with adversity become extremely important.

What a day! What a day! And it's not over. My walk today took me through the El Malpais lava flows.

The scenery in El Malpais lava flows was exquisite!

The geology of the New Mexico area is absolutely stunning. Almost as great as the people!

We got a little over twenty-two miles done today! Over half of it was without the brace, and I was still feeling pretty good.

I would not realize until after the trip was over that taking the brace off was a foolish idea. I did not realize it at that time, but the injury began a process of my right calf muscle starting to atrophy due to the injury. I noticed somewhere in the Texas and Oklahoma Panhandle and then into southwestern Kansas that I was dragging my right foot.

It was not so apparent until I began to feel the stones on the road that I was walking on with my right foot but not my left. I thought at first that it was because the blisters were on the right foot, but then I realized that the blisters were on the left foot.

My first inclination of a problem occurred when I realized I was wearing out the toe area on the front part of the right shoe. I tried all sorts of things to reinforce the shoe when perhaps it would have been better to find out why my shoes were wearing differently than they had in my entire life. This failure to notice the significance of that one minor issue would have significant consequences when I completed the walk. I just did not know it at that time.

I mention this because the decisions that you make and do not make have consequences. We may not understand it at that time, but you will realize it at some later date. We are all responsible for our actions.

Life Lessons Learned: **Small signs should not be ignored.**

April 24, 2014

With all the magnificent scenery, the day just flew by even though I noticed that I was getting tired. One cannot help finding humor everywhere when you are walking by yourself. As I was walking, I saw a pair of tennis shoes thrown over some electrical or phone wires. When I was a young parent, I would have been upset that some child acted that way. With my feet feeling the way they were, I thought I finally understood why someone would do that!

We made it over the last mountain today! A major hurdle has been overcome, and while I am still in the mountains east of Albuquerque, I am on the downhill until I get to Moriarty.

One of the things that I have noticed during this trip is how much I value friendship and family. I pray every day that our children at Good Shepherd will have a stable family life as well as great friends that will care about them forever. We have many children at Good Shepherd whose parents have been models of great parenting skills to be able to help their child get help when needed.

We also have children in our care whose parents never learned how to be a good parent. I started thinking about some of the challenges of parenthood. I realized that we do not get any training to become a parent, so our children will be affected by what happened to us as children.

Life Lessons Learned: **Our past shapes us. Breaking the cycle means breaking with the past while remembering it.**

Good family, like all this beautiful scenery around New Mexico, is just absolutely a wonderful gift from God.

April 25, 2014

Well, we did it! We are through the mountains. Well, we are through the mountains at least until I get to the Appalachian Mountains, but it is downhill for at least the next thousand miles. I was teasing on Facebook and told friends that I thought I could see Ocean City, Maryland, from here.

The scenery along Route 66 and New Mexico Route 333 were just breathtaking. I was not certain whether it was the adrenaline that was kicking in, but this was one of the first days where I really thought I was going to make the entire journey.

Little did I know that the rough days ahead would test my resolve.

I heard from a dear friend that I had not heard from since high school. Joanie Hatter Schreiber is an incredibly kind person with great compassion for all.

Joanie it's great to hear from you! It has been way too long!

> *Unfortunately once I get in the Oklahoma I'm converting to the northern route so I'll be going to Kansas, then St. Louis and then Indianapolis.*

> *Would love to See you when I get to Charleston again— FXR response to my high school classmate, Joanie Hatter.*

I tried something new with the ankle brace, and it seemed to work well because we got twenty-five miles done today. I did the first eighteen miles in the Rockies, so it was not just because of going into the Plains. What I did was rotate wearing it and not wearing it by stopping along the way and changing positions so that it did not rub against the heel of my foot and my ankle. I did not notice it at that time, but my right calf muscle was beginning to atrophy. Candidly, I was in God's hands and the protection of our Blessed Mother along the way.

I was walking near Moriarty, New Mexico, and I realized that from this point, I was going to be more affected by weather than by terrain!

April 26, 2014

The winds today were unbelievable. My apprehension that the walk was going to be more affected by weather rang true almost immediately.

> *The wind o' the wind!*

> *You have got to see this.*

We got twenty-two miles done today! Actually, I think I got sixty-nine miles done, but I was blown back by the wind forty-seven miles, so I only netted out 22!

It was surprisingly cold, and the winds were severe. I was surprised that this part of New Mexico was still over 6,200 feet. Actually, it was about one thousand feet higher than Albuquerque.

The extreme winds and the substantial gusts brought out a nice experience. I had five people pull over and ask me if I needed a ride because of the extreme gusts. The decency of people never ceased to amaze me.

I remembered while I was walking that my prayers for the next week would be devoted in large measure to my friends with the Order of Malta, who are leaving for our annual pilgrimage to Lourdes. During these pilgrimages, we are honored to take the sick, whom we call Malades, and their companions to Lourdes, France, for a week of prayer and healing.

The healing can be physical, but there is an abundance of spiritual healing. I have never had such peace in my life as when I was in the grotto in Lourdes. My devotion to our Blessed Mother became even more intense because of these journeys. Many of my non-Catholic friends have difficulty understanding the devotion Catholics have to our Blessed Mother.

We, as Catholics, worship only God: Father, Son, and Holy Spirit. We do love the mother of Jesus, who, by a special grace of God, was conceived without sin in view of the merits of his death on the cross. During this journey and when I was in Lourdes, my devotion to the Blessed Mother was magnified. I asked our Lady to intercede for me with her Son. Our Savior will honor the wishes of his mother! The comfort, when I was feeling so uncomfortable, was unimaginable.

The importance of motherhood and fatherhood was continuously reinforced to me during this journey. The examples of Saint Joseph and our Blessed Mother will guide us as parents.

Life Lessons Learned: **Our Blessed Mother is always with us to pray with us.**

I asked my friends on Facebook to pray for our Malades and pilgrims and the sick everywhere so that they will have a safe journey through life and a spiritual life as well.

April 27, 2014

I saw the following post on Facebook from Diana Ellis, who was an absolute godsend during this entire trip. She and her husband, Tae, and I became great friends. I always knew that I could call on them, but when I saw the following post, all I could think about was "Oh no, only 1,949 miles to go!"

> April 27, 2014 - Day #44 - Santa Rosa, NM - 857 miles down, 1949 left to go! 30.54% of the walk completed!

Today, I made it to Santa Rosa, New Mexico. We completed twenty-four miles for the day in some of the most ferocious winds I have ever seen! I was stunned, though, that I did not see one wind turbine!

I was very fortunate that all I had was the wind. This was the day that I heard about those wonderful folks in the Midwest who were experiencing tornadoes and sheer destruction. Praying for the tornado victims and their families became a primary goal for me today and the future weeks along with our Malades.

Now that I am through the mountains, I moved the base of operations to Santa Rosa for four days while I make up the miles between Moriarty and Santa Rosa. At that point on, I am on to Tucumcari before I head into Texas.

I knew the weather was going to be my greatest challenge after the mountains and perhaps the entire journey, but even with that realization, I had no idea that winds could get that ferocious. Even with these winds, I realized that the devastating winds of a tornado were three times greater than what was inconveniencing me, so my heart went out to the tornado victims. The winds around Wagon Wheel, New Mexico, knocked me off my feet!

Talk about a small world. I was in a restaurant in Moriarty, talking to a motorcycle rider about the winds we were both experiencing. He was commenting that he pulled over to get something to eat because he was getting blown all over the highway.

It turned out that he was a defense contractor, and he said he lived in Indianapolis. I suggested that he should meet a very dear friend of mine, Jim Sweeney. It turned out the motorcyclist and Jim were childhood buddies!

April 28, 2014

Once again I asked all to pray for all the victims and their families of the tornadoes. The victims of these tornadoes were on my mind the entire day and the rest of the journey. I made the following comment on Facebook:

> *Those winds were devastating!*
>
> *Help them during their time of rebuilding.*
>
> *God bless you all. Be careful with this weather as it moves east.*

I only got sixteen miles in because I had a three-hour ethics committee meeting, and I also had to head back to Albuquerque to renew the car lease for the support car. In order to sustain my other work, I had to stop periodically during the journey to handle matters at work, and the ethics committee meeting was one of them.

The hike was outstanding despite the winds. I was surprised about how hilly it is around Santa Rosa. It was quite beautiful, and the people that I met were even more wonderful.

I was excited about a site along the way today. I had a chance to see the blue hole, which is an unbelievably clear water source right in the middle of Santa Rosa. The blue hole is apparently part of the Carlsbad Caverns. I have never seen waters as crystal clear in such an incredibly dry area.

I was thinking of the value of persistence today when I was walking into the wind. Perhaps the winds were my wakeup call to be persistent in providing help to our children in need.

April 29, 2014

I received the following note from a supporter:

> *Curious as to when you started your journey? Me and my fiance are planning a 10000+ mile walk starting end of next month to bring awareness to the issues with homelessness in the country and to also promote love and peace towards all. We both wish you well and safe on the rest of your journey!*

When I saw her comment, I was excited for her and her fiancé. They will find the experience incredibly rewarding. Something as simple as walking and being with friends has more meaning than all the wealth in the world.

When I stopped to eat meals, everyone was talking about the devastation in the Midwest. I was saddened by the devastation. I have so many friends in the area, and I prayed for their safety. Little did I know that in the town of Greensburg, Kansas, which was previously devastated by an EF5 tornado, that I would meet people who would rescue me.

Life Lessons Learned: **God has a plan for your life. Enjoy the ride.**

After the walk was over, I looked back at all the things that happened that became prophetic of things that were to happen later on. God's hand in giving me experiences I needed challenged me to think of others first.

It was at this point that I realized that whenever I was selfish, I hurt others, and when I engaged in selfless sacrifice, I helped others. But I also realized that I only felt good when I was helping others. I regretted my sins and asked for forgiveness for those times in my life when I thought more about me than others. Today was one of those days. We have so much to be grateful for when we stop thinking about ourselves.

Life Lessons Learned: **A child pays for the sins of their parents.**

Life Lessons Learned: **A true leader leads by selfless sacrifice.**

That reflection caused me to write on Facebook:

> *I very seldom ask this but, if you are able, I would ask you to contribute financially to the tornado victims in the Midwest and in the south.*
>
> *If you are of the Catholic faith you can contact any of the dioceses in the areas affected or Catholic Charities.*

Other faiths have similar organizations such as the Lutheran Church, the Methodist Church, the Jewish faith, Presbyterian Church or the Baptist church and others.

Additionally you can consider the Red Cross as well.

If you are not able to contribute financially and are able to donate blood or clothing or things of that nature, I ask you to consider that as well.

This is now a time for all of us to work in unison to help people in need.

The winds today have finally died down.

In the past three days, the winds had been brutal. I had a seminal event. A seminal event is one of those times in your life when you are at a crossroads and you decide to do things differently.

Instead of praying that the winds die down, I asked for the strength to overcome the winds.

This realization happened when I met a biker going cross-county who buzzed past me the day before. I had breakfast with him and asked to have a picture taken with him and his partner, when I realized he was a double amputee, which was why he was riding the reclining bike. He did not speak English, but in the way of the road warriors, he understood my deep admiration for him and his persistence. He motivated me.

Obstacles have to be overcome, not wished away.

***Life Lessons Learned*: Obstacles are to be overcome, not wished away.**

We completed a little over twenty-five miles today. It's amazing what happens when there's no wind hitting you in the face!

Brian completed the second update, and it was wonderful talking to him. I found later in the week the interview posted on YouTube. This gave me a chance to hear from many friends who were following the journey.

Frank Ryan Walks Across America | April 29, 2014 | Update 2

Maryland Association of CPAs *member and* Business Learning Institute *instructor* Frank Ryan *is walking coast to coast to raise awareness for Good Shepherd Services. To learn more visit* http://followfrank.macpa.org/

In the midst of walking through New Mexico Frank stops to bring us up to date on his Walk Across America.

April 30, 2014

We completed another twenty-five miles today, and the weather was extremely cooperative. It was a wonderful time to pray and to think.

Here's a prayer of healing that I said along the way:

Lord, You invite all who are burdened to come to You.

Allow Your healing hand to help me.

Touch my soul with Your compassion for others.

Touch my heart with Your courage and infinite love for all.

Touch my mind with Your wisdom, that my mouth may always proclaim Your praise.

Teach me to reach out to You in my need, and help me to lead others to You by my example.

Most loving Heart of Jesus, bring me health in body and spirit that I may serve You with all my strength.

Touch it gently this life which You have created, now and forever. Amen. (Source: Imissal.com)

I thought so much of Saint Joseph as the example of the perfect dad. One of the special items I took with me on the journey across America was a beautiful relic of Saint Joseph given to me by my Rose Team from 2013 in Lourdes. It touched me so deeply because of how it reminded me of my dad and how much I missed him.

Whenever I started to think of the discomfort from walking, I thought of the wonderful sacrifices of Saint Joseph for his holy family. I knew that I did not live up to his expectations as a dad, but he served as an example for me to get better to help my own children.

As I looked at him holding his Son, I knew what I had to do for our children!

Received my first birthday greeting today! Awesome messages made me appreciate that folks cared.

From so many friends: "Happy Birthday Frank!"

May 1, 2014

On Facebook, I wrote,

> *First of all, thank you all so much for the birthday wishes. They made me feel so very special.*
>
> *I am on route 54 and I am heading to Tucumcari tomorrow. I will be on route 54 all the way into Kansas.*
>
> *For all my friends who have been affected by the rains and the tornadoes, you are in my prayers. I have been at Mass for the past two days and will be going tomorrow as well for your intentions.*
>
> *I found that going to Mass was so comforting. To be in prayer with so many faithful and to meet with our priests and to have our walk prayer petitions blessed was an awesome experience.*
>
> *I thought today of Father Bill Kuchinsky, Father Rodrigo Arroyo, and Father Alexander Drummond, Msgr Dillon and all the other great priests I have met in my lifetime and thank God that these men were so willing to sacrifice so much to be our spiritual fathers on earth.*

We completed almost twenty-six miles today, and the weather was mostly cooperative, although some of the skies were getting pretty threatening. Every time I would see threatening skies, I wondered if this was it, meaning a tornado forming. Only when I reached Kansas and Missouri and all the way through Indiana did I finally understand what a tornado looks like. It is amazing what a little experience teaches!

Life Lessons Learned: **An inquisitive mind allows experiences to expand your horizons.**

As I was walking, I saw beautiful, sunny skies. When I turned around, I saw a completely different situation relative to threatening weather. It was a very powerful reminder of being careful when I go into western Oklahoma and Kansas and farther east. What you see ahead of you may not reflect what is behind you.

One of the reasons that this walk across America is so important to me came about because of a friend of mine, Skip Counselman.

Skip introduced me to the Order of Malta and recommended me for membership.

As part of the Order of Malta program, you are required to do a year of formation. In that formation, you are required to be active in the order and not just give money.

Helping others is about helping them and not just always writing a check.

Skip, let me thank you from the bottom of my heart (and my feet! ☺).

May 2, 2014

All in all, today was an outstanding day! I had first-Friday Mass at Saint Rosa of Lima Parish in Santa Rosa. It was great to see so many parents and children at the first-Friday Mass.

The staff at the Super 8 Motel was intrigued by the mission of the Good Shepherd Services. There were really good people there.

We moved our base of operations today to Tucumcari, New Mexico.

I continued my walking on Route 54 / Route 66. It was interesting to see the nostalgia in this part of New Mexico. Some of the vehicles reminded me of days long ago.

I was thinking about how we approach helping children with behavioral, emotional, and developmental disabilities and hoping that nostalgia does not get in the way of new and more effective treatments. The staff and the Sisters of the Good Shepherd are always looking for compassionate and considerate ways of helping children.

It is interesting to watch the way some of the towns on the old Route 66 have been abandoned. I was going to stop in Cuervo, New Mexico, but the town is a ghost town now. Other spots along Route 66 have been restored, but whole other areas have been rendered obsolete because of the interstate.

Many areas were just not able to deal with the changing technology— somewhat sad for the people affected and why the abandonment happened in the first place. It was a most sobering experience, particularly as I began to see more and more abandoned or dying towns along the way. The expression about having to change to survive has new meaning for me.

Life Lessons Learned: **The status quo is no longer an option. Grow or be rendered obsolete.**

May 3, 2014

While I was walking, the trains along my path kept me company. They were to become a very familiar sight for over one thousand miles of the journey. I felt as if I were not so isolated when they went by. Because it was the same track for most of the distance, I even began to recognize some of the locomotives, and it seemed like some of the crews. I had company!

I am still walking! But God works in mysterious ways!

I was heading to dinner tonight and ran into Tom McNamara. Tom was taking pictures, and I was concerned about bumping into him, so I said "Excuse me" as I was passing him.

We started to talk, and I told them I was walking across America. He seemed a little incredulous, and he said, "Really?"

I went on to explain how I was doing it for emotionally, behaviorally, and/or developmentally disabled children for the Sisters of the Good Shepherd.

He seemed genuinely intrigued and explained that he was distributing socks to homeless people and had distributed 1,500 socks in the past four days.

We agreed to meet at Mass tomorrow at 10:30 at Saint Anne's in Tucumcari.

I told him that if we are successful, maybe he will not need to keep distributing socks in the future. Do not underestimate the value of those socks. The homeless (and those walking across America) came to cherish the socks. Wow, I had no idea how cherished socks would become. Homeless people mentioned that all the time. Socks and shoes.

It was a pleasure meeting Tom, my newfound friend!

We completed a little over twenty-five miles, which put me pretty close to one thousand miles. What a milestone, no pun intended.

My feet are holding up better than I expected, and the temperatures are starting to climb again!

For some reason, I met a lot of people today who were very interested in our mission at Good Shepherd. Everyone seemed to really care.

Also, the drought here, like for most of the area where I have walked so far, is a major problem and is creating untold problems. I saw a dust vortex for the first time since being in Afghanistan and Iraq and was surprised about the dried-up rivers and lakes.

May 4, 2014

We made it to Logan, New Mexico, although the issue was in doubt!

The temperature hit ninety-eight degrees. The heat was very similar to the temperatures when I started my walk in California. Lately, though, the temperatures have been around forty-five to fifty degrees, which has been ideal for walking, except for those days when the winds were over fifty miles an hour. The swing in daily temperatures caused me to have to carry more gear because of the need to change clothing as the temperature changed.

Each day, my good friend Greg Conderacci would send me an e-mail called Today's Thought. They were always wonderful reflections and served as a basis for my prayers for the day.

Today's thought was this:

> *Flowers unfold slowly and gently, bit by bit in the sunshine, and a soul to must never be punished were driven, but unfolds in its own perfect timing to reveal its true wonder and beauty. (The Findhorn Community)*

Because of Greg's quote, I began to think about the value of Christ's love and his ability to forgive without holding a grudge. Wouldn't it be wonderful if all of us could forgive and truly forgive! Keep praying for that ideal.

Life Lessons Learned: **Forgiveness, like love, must be unconditional.**

I entered into the Great Plains around Logan, New Mexico. The flatness is a little deceiving because of the gently rolling hills, but the area is still very much a high desert area. The drought is having a profound effect on the entire southwestern part of the United States. I am beginning to understand how the dust bowl occurred during the Great Depression.

Despite the drought, the people have been wonderful. Their resilience in the face of hardship underlies a tremendous faith. I was somewhat surprised that during my time in New Mexico, the strength of the faith of the people I met along the way. I was honored to be able to spend this Easter season with them.

I have some regret, though, about leaving New Mexico on Tuesday.

New Mexico, California, and Arizona were so perfect because I was blessed to meet so many great folks.

I got twenty-six miles done but had to try a little different training regiment because of the heat during the day. I walked until about 3:00 PM and then took a break from 3:00 PM until 5:00 PM. After 5:00 PM, I started walking again and got done at 10:00 PM. I am a little apprehensive of how this will work out in terms of getting food and sleep, but time will tell.

It is projected to be one hundred degrees again tomorrow! Thank God it's a dry heat! We used that expression in the military in the desert during the short time I was in Afghanistan and while I was in Iraq. If you do not keep up your sense of humor, these minor challenges become obstacles. Keep a light heart, stay focused in prayer, and stay optimistic.

May 5, 2014

There was a whole bunch of stuff going on today!

First, I made it through New Mexico! I am now in Texas—the Lone Star State.

I have been impressed with everyone that I met in New Mexico. This feeling has become a recurring theme. I was starting to lose my cynicism because of such great people. We often hear only bad news, and so when you see that what you are hearing and what you are seeing and experiencing are two different things, you cannot help but question what you have heard.

Life Lessons Learned: **Do not always believe what you read. Believe in people.**

I have noticed that many of the smaller towns in Quay County in New Mexico are suffering because of the Interstate 40 bypass and some industries have left town. Despite that adversity, the people remain very optimistic, compassionate, and friendly.

I got over twenty-six miles in today. At the same time, I lost an hour because I crossed into the central time zone. I did not realize that losing that one hour would be such a big deal. But it cut an hour out of my walk time for the next day, and I was starting to get into the groove of walking twenty-five miles per day. It was not a big deal, but I was surprised that I did notice it the next day.

The funniest part of the day was that at about 6:00 PM, I realized I had not eaten since breakfast. I was starting to get rundown. I had a quick sandwich and was up and running to get the twenty-six miles done. Amazing what a little fuel does! The euphoria of the phenomenal experiences I had occasionally caused me to forget certain very important issues like eating.

Life Lessons Learned: **Value food, sleep, and peaceful times.**

Forgetting to eat became a potential problem later on. I did not realize that you can fall into a sense of routine in walking. The physical demands are anything but routine when you are doing this type of walk over a prolonged period. One starts to take important tasks for granted because you are not feeling any major physical stress as you would with an activity that was more physically demanding. There comes a certain point at which your body crashes from the lack of food. Once you begin to crash, things snowball.

I found myself getting caught up with the people and the scenery and took some important tasks for granted.

> May 5, 2014 - Day #52 - TX - 1053 miles down, 1753 left to go! 37.53% of the walk completed!

May 6, 2014

Today was a particularly difficult day. I posted this on Facebook:

> *I may need to ask you to pray that the winds die down. I've completed 18 miles so far and I'm not done for the day but when I was walking today the winds kicked up more ferociously than I've seen in my entire 50 some days of the walk.*

> *It reminds me of the perseverance that we have to have in order to accomplish our mission so that we can take care of our children. Regardless of the obstacles we have to keep moving forward.*

The Stronger we are as a team, working together, the more
we can help our kids overcome their obstacles.

I was pretty certain that once I got out of the Rockies the
big issue is going to be the weather. This is one of the few
times that I am sorry that I am right. ☺

**Life Lessons Learned: Overcoming obstacles sets a new standard to
help overcome the next obstacle.**

I received some great messages while I was walking. It made the
challenges of the day much easier to deal with. I made a comment to
my dear friend Sue Rodkey:

Sue you don't know how much that means to me. After
I took this video the winds really kicked up and I was
pushing a cart or should I say the winds were pushing me
and I was trying to hold onto the court! :-)

Something strange happened today. It explains why and how we should
trust in God's plan for us. We may not always understand what God's
plan is, but we should trust in him.

I screwed up.

Allow me set the stage!

First, I was making great progress for the first eleven miles. Then the
winds kicked up. They were brutal! Winds were not as bad as they were
seven or eight days ago, but what made these worse was because I was
using a cart to carry some of my gear.

The aerodynamics of the cart made it like a parachute, which was
pushing opposite the direction I was going. My times declined to about
1.5 miles per hour, and the temperature was still well over ninety
degrees.

I was getting hot and cranky!

To make matters less comfortable, the backward motion of the winds from the direction I was going caused me to get more blisters on my feet. This was because of the friction of being pulled in two different directions. Nothing serious with the blisters, but just frustrating since my feet had just recovered from the last episode.

The counteractions with the winds also wore out another pair of shoes.

So this is now where trusting in God's plan comes to pass.

I decided to walk to the Sears store to see if I could find shoes. Remember that I was in a rural community, so shoe stores were not everywhere. The young lady at Sears was so nice to refer me to the tractor supply store.

On the way to get shoes, I decided to stop in and get Blistex to help my feet. At the United Food store, I met Debbie and Sean.

We started talking about the mission of Good Shepherd Services, and Sean thought I should talk to the local newspaper reporter about our mission and the walk. Sean put us on contact with one another, and we finished talking with Joe from the local newspaper about our mission.

So as a result of all my complaining, God's plan really had me meet well over fifteen people that I had the chance to talk to about our mission. These were people I would not have met otherwise.

Life Lessons Learned: **Trust in God's plan. Everything happens for a reason.**

At sixty-three years of age, you would think I would know that by now.

All was good, but I needed that wakeup call.

I met some outstanding people in Dalhart. This is a community with great community values. I am thankful that Christ led me here.

Tomorrow's winds are supposed to be ferocious, so I am not sure how much I will get done, but I will be going into the wind with a different attitude!

May 7, 2014

Good news :(. Wind advisory just declared for Dalhart today!

Oh joy! I love a challenge. (You can read sarcasm into that if you would like.) ☺

Seriously, I looked forward to the challenge because it gave me a better perspective of what our children go through daily.

There was also so great news on two accounts.

First, my dear friend Col. Doug Sethness, Green Beret, who was chief of staff of the Joint Forces Special Operations Command during Operation Enduring Freedom, joined me on the walk today and would be with me for the next couple days.

Second, I ran into a fantastic marine family when I went to get my haircut.

All in all, a great military day! And the winds were fantastic and gave me a great chance to learn.

Completed 25.2 miles and had Doug Sethness help me with a support vehicle for the last nine miles. Doug walked with me as well over the next few days.

The winds were severe today but manageable. You should have seen the dust storms that came about.

I am beginning to appreciate how quickly weather can change and how I need to be very careful. As I was walking, it was extraordinarily hot. The skies ahead of me were cloudless and with the most majestic blue color you could imagine. But then I noticed it went from being extremely hot to relatively cool. I turned around to be greeted with angry-looking clouds building into thunderstorms.

I was expecting full-blown rainstorms, but I realized that this area was still suffering from a severe drought and the rain and thunderstorms potential was still at least four days away. It did give me a wakeup call, though, that I needed to be prepared with gear and contingency plans should I get caught outdoors in fairly isolated areas with no coverage should a tornado occur.

May 8, 2014

Well, we did it!

Just crossed over into Oklahoma! My short stay in Texas was outstanding, and I met more wonderful folks. Just as I expected!

It was a great day for walking even though I finished at 10:30 PM.

It was great having Doug Sethness with me. Great friend and great patriot!

In just three days in Texas, I have met so many incredibly fantastic people.

From Dalhart to Stratford to Texhoma, the compassion and concern of so many wonderful people were apparent everywhere. I am incredibly optimistic about the people of this country.

May 9, 2014

What an absolutely beautiful day to be walking. Completed twenty-five more miles and made it a little bit past Guymon, Oklahoma. Got here just in time for bike week!

I stopped at a restaurant in the panhandle of Oklahoma and met two wonderful folks, Jo and Crystal, who were very supportive of our efforts at Good Shepherd.

We also ran into a little critter on the side of the road, which was about a three-and-half-foot-long snake. I am not a big fan of snakes. People who know me will call that the understatement of the year. Having seen so many snakes by now, though, I have gotten used to them.

I started to see green, which was a nice change from what I had experienced thus far in the trip because of the drought. This part of Oklahoma is also suffering from the same drought conditions that the entire Southwest is feeling, but they are able to use irrigation systems for the crops and cattle.

May 10, 2014

I was honored to have Doug with me for the past two and a half days. Doug is a true patriot, but that word does not suffice for him. Doug and I got to know each other during some extremely stressful periods in our nation's history. We were working days well in excess of twenty hours per day for prolonged periods and having to make critical decisions simultaneously.

Fatigue can take its toll, and sometimes judgments can become clouded. Doug and I were faced with a fairly challenging task that was not popular, and despite personal risk to him, he made the right decision, which I think had a favorable effect on the safety of thousands of young men and women in Afghanistan. Doug displayed that type of moral courage that should serve as an example for all of us. He did the right thing at the right time for the right reason regardless of the personal impact on him.

I will miss having you with me on this trip, but I am thankful for the great time we spent together.

***Life Lessons Learned*: Do the right thing at the right time for the right reason—moral courage.**

Doug is heading back home as I prepare to leave to teach for two days in Las Vegas. There is this funny thing called income that is very helpful to support the habit of walking across America! Seriously, I have agreed to lecture with CPAs six to ten days during this journey to help defray the costs of the trip. It was important to me that all the expenses of this trip be mine and that any money raised go to the children.

While walking in the Oklahoma Panhandle, Suzanne, the spouse of the commissioner of Texas County, Oklahoma, stopped and was very helpful and cordial in helping us make the rest of the trip this week bearable.

I am very close to the Kansas border and still believe that people care about solving our problem with how to help children with emotional and behavioral problems.

My optimism builds every day.

I return to the panhandle of Oklahoma and then Kansas on Wednesday.

We completed twenty-one miles today. I ended a little early since I had to drive back to Albuquerque tomorrow morning, which is a six-hour drive, to fly to my class.

I saw a campaign sign today: "Elder for state representative." It reminded me of Jennifer Elder and her husband, Sam, who are good friends of mine. I sent her a note and said that apparently she was not aware that she was running for state representative in Oklahoma!

Sue Rodkey asked me if I sang the song "Oklahoma" while there. You have to understand, I have probably one of the worst singing voices in the world, which most people who know me are aware of. I said to Sue, "Sue, I did sing Oklahoma! The state police of Oklahoma then escorted me to Kansas! :-)"

I remember when I was in grade school that our class was rehearsing songs for Mass, and in a crowd of sixty students, one of the sisters pointed me out and gently reminded me that I can praise God just as much by moving my lips! Ouch!

May 11, 2014

I left Guymon, Oklahoma, at 4:30 AM to go to Albuquerque for my flight to Las Vegas. The support vehicle I was using had to be returned to Albuquerque, and it was the closest airport to where I was going to be. The trip was expected to take over six hours.

As I was driving back, it occurred to me that I was covering in six hours what had taken me almost fifteen days to walk.

In thinking about that, it came to mind about how efficient six hours of driving was compared to walking. Then I thought about the wonderful memories that I had in the fifteen days that I would not have gotten covering the same distance at seventy miles per hour.

If you have the chance, slow down and enjoy the scenery of life along the way.

Life Lessons Learned: The goal in life is not speed. Our founding fathers did not have a computer when they wrote the Constitution.

To moms and stepmoms everywhere, happy Mother's Day!

Remember, the Blessed Mother is the mother of the entire universe.

May 11, 2014 - Day #58 - Guymon, OK - 1187 miles down, 1619 left to go! 42.29% of the walk completed!

I completed my trek back to Albuquerque to drop off the car and then fly to Las Vegas.

We were still able to get eleven miles in today but in six different locations!

I had two wonderful experiences today.

First was the Mass in Moriarty, New Mexico, and the incredibly warm reception that I received there.

What stunned me the most was the absolute generosity, kindness, and sincere warmth toward our mission by a young person at the restaurant at the Tropicana Hotel in Las Vegas. Her name was Jorin. You could see the compassion toward our girls and boys in her eyes, and her generosity and kindness were overwhelming.

If you ever doubt whether or not there are good people in the world, please let me know, because I will convince you that there are more good people than you can possibly imagine.

May 12, 2014

I leave Las Vegas tomorrow and head back to Oklahoma to continue our journey.

I did get some good miles in today, which surprised me, but I had to get resupplied since this was one of the few cities I could get the gear that I need.

I was so grateful for the kind reception I received at the Tropicana and some of the stores in Las Vegas from people who were very helpful because they cared!

I think this is where my cynicism died! I never expected such wonderful attitudes from so many folks in such a busy city. We just need to look for good!

At Mass during my trip to Las Vegas, I talked to a monsignor who was heading up the Las Vegas HIV center, and I was so impressed at his love of his mission in life. His compassion for those in need was extraordinary.

May 14, 2014

The MACPA and Blue Ocean Ideas team, Brian, talked to me today, and it was a great time to reconnect with him and friends back home. I have so much to be grateful for. Tom Hood, the executive director of the MACPA and a true thought leader for our CPA profession, was so kind to offer to publicize the walk and our children.

> *Frank Ryan's* Walk Across America *marches on. Here's another update from Frank and the* Blue Ocean Ideas *team.*
>
> *Well we did it!*
>
> *We entered Kansas and left Oklahoma.*
>
> *Due to road construction, the Kansas state sign is down.*

The realization that I crossed the panhandle of Texas and Oklahoma in about a week compared to fifty days to go through three states motivated me. I knew that I had to cross fourteen states, and when it takes you fifty days to get through three, the end of the walk seems almost unattainable.

The thought was going through my mind that at this rate, I would not get done until December. But when I crossed two states so quickly and got into Kansas, the realization hit that we were making progress. I could see the finish line even though it was still 1,400 miles away.

I never doubted for a second that we would finish the walk. I did doubt whether or not I would get it done this decade though!

Next state, Missouri, is only 340 miles away!

For those who do not know me, I am fairly conservative, and tomorrow I am heading into Liberal, Kansas, and posted this:

> *By the way I'm wondering if I'm going to be allowed to enter into Liberal, Kansas tomorrow?*
>
> *I forgot to bring my Passport with me. I wonder if I can get an interpreter at the city limits?*

Well, that comment got some feedback!

Karl Ahlrichs sent me a note about whether or not I was seeing green. He kept in close contact when I was walking and often remarked that the drought was so severe that all I saw was brown. This change in scenery was really nice. I told him that I expected to see green on a regular basis by tomorrow afternoon.

Just think about that for a second. Seeing green created almost a feeling of euphoria, things that I took for granted!

I also got a message from my cousin, although she calls me Uncle Frank. Amanda Sedlak is the daughter of my cousin Jeanne Marie. Jeanne Marie is actually more like a sister to me, and we are very close. Amanda is a wonderful person, and she is getting married shortly to Patrick Billman, who is proudly serving in the United States Army. They are currently in the Kansas City area, so I was hoping that we would be able to meet later on in the journey. It was wonderful to break bread with this newly married couple.

It is a great day walking. I can feel the effects of being at lower altitudes. I am at about three thousand feet, and the strength and endurance have returned to what I normally experienced before I started this walk.

May 15, 2014

> May 15, 2014 - Day #62 - Liberal, KS - 1233 miles down, 1573 left to go! 43.93% of the walk completed!
> — with Frank Ryan.

I finally found a Welcome to Kansas sign! Diana Ellis was pretty specific with me that I had better not return home without taking pictures of the signs of the states I had gone through. Since I did not have one from California and did not think about it in entering Arizona, I thought she would let me off the hook, but no, not Diana! Seriously, it started as a request but ended up being a huge help while chalking up the miles. Great midway points to recharge the batteries and to see the progress.

Unbelievable day today!

For the second time on my journey, I have run into someone on the route for a second time.

Today I was walking just to the west of Meade, Kansas, and I was stopped by a gentleman who asked me how I was doing. At first, I was a little surprised, and then it dawned on me that we had met in Texas. He asked me if I remembered him from Dalhart, Texas, and I said that I had. It was so nice to have someone take the time out and say hello. It made me feel as if the message of the walk was working.

Life Lessons Learned: **Every person you meet is important regardless of their position in life. Act accordingly.**

The second thing that happened was right outside of Liberal, Kansas. I saw a gentleman who was walking. You could tell he was down on his luck. I was combating whether or not I should do something to help other than just talk to him to see how he was doing. I finally decided it was important to help even if I thought it might be misused. I thought about that all day.

It was a constant battle in my mind about whether or not I did the right thing.

Well, the Blessed Mother and our Savior had an answer for me by the end of the day.

I stopped for the night in Kansas. As I was walking to get something to eat, this gentleman jumped out of the car because he had gotten a ride from a farmer in the area. He seemed genuinely excited to see someone who had cared about him earlier in the day.

The farmer and I and the gentleman talked for a little bit, and the farmer said the most telling comment, I think, when he said "This could be us."

Life Lessons Learned: **We are all only one life event away from being in total need.**

I needed to remember that we never know when we will see our Savior. Once we are born, time is not on our side.

It reminded me of a person in the store called Travel Plus in Las Vegas who went out of his way to find me equipment that I needed. His advice made my trip that much easier. He cared!

That is all we need to do for our children—care for them and love them.

Got a little bit over twenty-five miles done today! Starting tomorrow, the weather is going to be a little bit less cooperative, although it did drizzle a little today.

Heather McGinnity of Myers & Stauffer in Maryland posted an unbelievable picture of the firm, wishing me well. The impact of that message was huge, particularly in light of what was going to happen in the next few days. Like so many other events that happened during this trip, the picture from Heather and the Stauffer & Myers team recharged my batteries and my spirit to keep forging ahead.

Heather McGinnity   *4:19 pm May 15*

I have been in the audience of several of Frank's presentations through the MACPA and he is a motivating leader. My coworkers and I are inspired by this tremendous journey and wanted to share that with Frank and all his followers.

Regards,
Heather McGinnity, CPA
Myers & Stauffer

It turned out that it appeared as if Facebook removed the picture, but as I was to find out later, it just got "pushed down" for some unknown reason. I could see that it was there, but Heather could not. We finally figured out what it was so that all could see.

May 16, 2014

I started the day in Meade, then went to Fowler, and ended up in Minneola, Kansas.

The trend of meeting great folks continues unabated.

Reminded me of a sign I saw today on a grain elevator. It said "Co-op." Imagine what we could accomplish if we all cooperated to help solve the problem of how to help our children. What a great thought!

I saw a train bridge today that was made only out of wood. The load was distributed to bear the weight of the train. That is exactly what came to mind about how we could distribute the load of having the greatest amount of help for our children if we work together. Imagine what we could do.

Life Lessons Learned: **Workload distributed is bearable. Acting alone leads to failure.**

I met a person who was riding his bike, and he heard that I was walking across the nation. He stopped to talk to find out what our mission was about.

On somewhat of a funny aside, by the time I was done walking, it went from being very calm outside to sustained winds of thirty to forty miles an hour. Being in Kansas, I kept looking for Toto.

We had a great day in that we got twenty-seven miles in, but the last two miles took me one hour! In that one hour, though, we had a chance to talk to more people about our mission. It was probably one of the most productive hours I have had.

May 17, 2014

It was another unbelievable day.

It started yesterday when I arrived in Minneola. I was on target to get a great deal of miles. I went to eat, and I realized there was only one restaurant in town.

Everything worked out fairly well at dinner, and I met two truck drivers and struck up a conversation about Good Shepherd.

The town had been hit so hard because of the economy that there were no restaurants open for breakfast, and there was only one hotel in the entire town as well.

I had not slept too well last night and started out on my walk without eating.

Before I left on my second leg of the walk this morning, I ran into one of the two truck drivers, and he wished us well and was truly compassionate about the limping that I was experiencing with my right leg. He gave me some great advice on some emu oil to help with the knees. He was very concerned.

After that, I walked another eight miles before I realized I was just too tired to go on without eating.

I stopped at Bucklin Café and C-Store. I met a group of people that were interested in our mission. I was explaining that I was just a little tuckered out but motivated to keep moving on, but deep down, I knew I was in trouble. I was not sure I had the strength to go on any farther despite my positive words to the contrary.

The waitress told me that as I head out on my journey, that if I get tired again, just to remember to always have faith. I said that I did, but she looked at me with that wise stare as if she knew I was exhausted. She then repeated, "Have faith."

Little did she know that in addition to the great menu items, they also served up heaping helpings of faith, hope, and charity. She gave me the motivation I needed to move forward. From that day forward, I never questioned finishing the walk.

As I continued walking for a total of twenty-six miles, I was easily stopped fifteen to twenty times by people concerned as to whether I needed a ride. With each one of them, I told the story and mission of Good Shepherd.

One person, Chris, told me about the passing of his grandmother, and I promised that I would pray for her and his family this week.

Then I got to Greensburg, Kansas, where the city had been totally destroyed by an EF5 tornado on May 4, 2007. This town is the most resilient town I have seen in my life. It was touching to see such a positive attitude for people so deeply affected by such a horrible tragedy.

At the end of the day, I had dinner, and a Mennonite man by the name of Lloyd came up and talked to me about our faith-based mission. What a man of Christ!

This day pumped me up more than you can ever possibly imagine, and these tired old bones were ready to go on.

I sent this message in response to a post from Denni Barton Rehmer, whose daughter was the waitress at breakfast:

> *Thank you for telling me about your daughter. I was so touched by her kindness that I went back to try to get a picture of her and the other people at the restaurant but they'd already left for the day. You should be incredibly proud of her. Her faith gave me a shot of adrenaline that helped me make it through the day—Mother is Denni Barton Rehmer.*

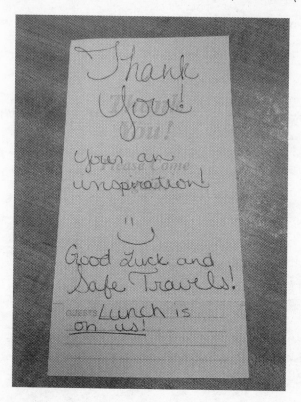

Denni's daughter had a bigger impact on me than you can imagine. You see, I was exhausted when I went into the restaurant. I thought I was ready to quit. To say that I was hurting is putting it mildly. As I sat down for breakfast, the thought of disappointing our children was becoming a reality. I had no more reserves, or so I thought.

But then this angel at the Bucklin Café and C-Store stepped up and, with great compassion in her eyes, told me to "have faith." I thought about what she said that the picture of encouragement I received from my friends at Stauffer & Myers as well as what Tom Hood had done with CPAs in Western Maryland, and the discomfort became bearable.

From that moment on, finishing the walk was never going to be an issue. I realized that it may not look pretty, but it was going to happen. I was in God's hands, plain and simple.

Life Lessons Learned: **Just because you do not know that your kindness has made an impression, it has.**

May 18, 2014

I went to Mass in Pratt, Kansas, at Sacred Heart Parish, which is the same name as my parish in Cornwall, Pennsylvania. I thought about my wonderful parish priest, Father Rodrigo Arrazola, and the great spiritual leadership he provides for us. A true man of Christ! All was good!

After Mass, I began walking from Minneola, and it was in the high thirties to low forties and pretty cold. The fog was like a sheer wall. I could not see more than about one hundred feet ahead. I was a little concerned about safety, but the walking area near the road was pretty wide. Yet in just four hours, the temperature was almost ninety degrees and the sun was shining brightly.

The challenge of packing gear for these types of changes was interesting. I never knew what gear to bring since weather changed so often.

From Minneola, I continued walking to Greensburg, Kansas, and I wrote,

> *I hope you are as proud of the people of Greensburg Kansas as I am.*
>
> *Pray for their continued recovery.*
>
> *Very somber experience.*
>
> *From Bucklin to Greensburg to Pratt Kansas, the spirit of these communities is testimony to their unrelenting faith.*
>
> *I have been mesmerized with the spirit in these communities since Bucklin.*
>
> *I spent a good bit of the day, after mass in Pratt at Sacred Heart Church, in the town of Greensburg.*
>
> *Seeing the pictures of the devastation from the EF5 tornado in 2007 to the vacant lots in the town, the hospitality, kindness, and the faith of this community were remarkable.*

I saw the same thing in Bucklin, and I am sure it exists throughout this part of Kansas and perhaps the entire state.

As I was told in Bucklin yesterday to just have faith, I am convinced that our faith must guide us and be unwavering.

So to the folks in Bucklin to Greensburg to Pratt, thank you so much for the wonderful reminder of our faith.

From folks stopping to offer me water because I was on the road, to the two wonderful people at the Big Well center in downtown Greensburg, to the waitress at the Bucklin Café, thank you for reminding me about our need for faith.

Both of the folks at the Big Well center, by the way, survived the tornado.

Just amazing!

May 19, 2014

I love playing jokes and decided to have some fun with my good friend Skip Counselman, whose birthday was soon. On Facebook, I said,

> *Sometimes I think it is just wrong to put on a public social media site that it's someone's birthday.*
>
> *I want you all to know that I have no intention of putting on this site tomorrow that it is Skip Counselman's birthday tomorrow.*
>
> *It is important to me that I maintain that standard. :)*
>
> *Happy birthday Skip! Tomorrow that is.*

Skip and his wife, Margie, are two of those people who are always giving of themselves. Skip is the reason I am with the Order of Malta. He and I served together on the Saint Agnes Hospital board of directors when he was chairman. Skip is one of those persons who will never have to question whether or not they made a difference.

As I was walking today, my father-in-law's health began to deteriorate rapidly. I thought of the great sacrifice that Sherrie made to allow me to do this walk when her dad was so ill. I prayed for him and her and her mom and their family every day.

> *Sherrie's dad is gravely ill. His name is John Costa and he is a great person.*
>
> *Many people have lost hope but I still believe in the power of miracles.*
>
> *Please pray John Costa and his entire family in this their time of need.*

Life Lessons Learned: Believe in miracles. Never give up.

While I have not completed walking for the day yet and was hoping to get a total of twenty-five miles in, I thought about persistence and hope.

When you think about persistence, you need to think about the walk today and about my brother Bob.

I started out the day doing most of my walk in Haviland, Kansas, and ended up in Pratt, Kansas. The scenery was absolutely beautiful, but the temperature difference from the start of the morning to the end of the day was unbelievable.

The temperature started out at about forty-five degrees and ended up so far near ninety-five degrees. The winds were a significant crosswind of about twenty-five to thirty miles per hour sustained with gusts up to about thirty-five to forty miles per hour.

The truck traffic was pretty heavy.

The winds in and of themselves—no problem.

The trucks in and of themselves—no problem.

The temperature with some judgment—no problem.

You put the temperature, the trucks, and the crosswinds together and you have one interesting day!

But we made it. Just like my brother Bob made it. He was notified today that after taking sixteen weeks of training and extensive testing, he is now a certified fireman. He's doing it as a volunteer, which is not bad for someone who is sixty-seven years old.

My brother Bob has always been my hero. He was never afraid to take chances, and he built a very successful business. He had been in retirement for a while when he decided to become a volunteer fireman.

Persistence like my brother Bob's is what will help us overcome any obstacle that we may have in caring for our children.

Our faith, hope, charity, and persistence and devoting our lives and doing for others before ourselves—this is a recipe for great success in our mission.

Way to go, brother Bob. Proud of you!

I had a good day, but I also remembered some very hard-learned lessons that I almost forgot and could have paid a price for. Thank God for prayers and prayers being answered.

First, on top of the seventeen-plus miles yesterday, we got twenty-eight miles today.

But the real lesson learned is not to cut corners. I did that today and almost paid a price for it.

***Life Lessons Learned*: The road with a shortcut may be a road to disaster.**

After the first four miles, I went out to do five more miles. I was doing the miles in Haviland, near Barclay College.

I got distracted when I was leaving the support vehicle and forgot to take any water with me. The wind was coming from the south, so it was a pretty strong crosswind and the temperature was fairly cool. The impact of not having water was a big deal at this point. Water is always important, but with the cooler temperatures and winds, I took a shortcut.

However, within an hour and a half, the temperature went from fifty degrees to the low nineties, and by the time I realized how warm it was, I was already three miles outside of town and becoming dehydrated. At that point, I decided to go back and get water and reposition the car.

By then, though, the full effects of dehydration from earlier in the day kicked in.

I was so intent upon getting the twenty-five miles done that I ignored the temperature and no water initially and continued for another total of nine miles. Big mistake.

At this point, it was in the ninety-five- to ninety-seven-degree temperature range, and I was becoming severely dehydrated despite having had some water. When I was training for this walk, I tried to deliberately see what heat exhaustion felt like, and I trained to combat it. I could tell this time I was getting close to heat exhaustion. The water I had on me was hot, so it was of limited value to drink.

What I decided to do was use the remaining water to splash on my face and on the scarf around my neck so that the wind kept me cool. That did the trick.

The message is, don't cut corners.

May 20, 2014

Maggie Esselman posted on Walk Across America's timeline:

> *You have been an inspiration to me since the first time I met you. You continue to amaze me. My prayers are with you every day, every step of the way. If anyone can accomplish this, you can do it. God bless you, every step of the way.*

Such words of encouragement from Maggie gave me a real boost much like food to nourish the spirit to continue the journey for a cause much bigger than me.

We are on our way to Hutchinson, Kansas, and head out on Wednesday for a two-day lecture assignment in Santa Fe, New Mexico, to help defray the expenses of the trip.

On leaving Pratt, Kansas, though, I saw a few signs that I thought were pretty interesting. I love a city with a sense of humor. There were two water towers side by side: one said "Hot" and the other "Cold." I was laughing so hard from this that I was sure people would stop to see if I had lost it!

We started walking around Hutchinson today.

We completed twenty-five miles! Due to the heat, I altered my walk schedule, so I did fourteen miles in the morning before 11:00 AM and then did the remaining miles after 4:00 PM.

The prairie dogs were a blast to watch. They have neat personalities. Their chirps send a warning signal to all the other holes. As I walked by, they came out and followed me until the next one took over.

May 21, 2014

I arrived in Santa Fe to lecture for two days. I kept walking to keep loose and completed ten miles, part on the Santa Fe Trail.

Santa Fe is a gorgeous city, and while here, it was a great time to pray for all our intentions on our prayer walk of atonement and gratitude.

I also encourage you to pray to the Blessed Mother to intercede for you to carry your special petitions to our Savior, Jesus Christ.

On my travel from Hutchinson to the Kansas City airport, I had a chance to see where I would be walking over the next eight days after I got back, and I was excited!

Thank you all for your good wishes during the trip and for your prayers for John Costa.

John is struggling this evening, and I ask you for your continued prayers. I believe in miracles!

May 23, 2014

I saw this message on Facebook today:

> *Frank has completed 50% of the Walk Across America!*
> *1408 miles down . . . 1398 left to go! Way to go, Frank.*

First, I want to thank everyone for their prayers for Sherrie's dad and my father-in-law, John Costa.

I was returning from Albuquerque to Kansas to resume my walk, and I was notified that John passed away at 9:00 PM this evening.

I would ask you to please keep him and his entire family in your prayers during this time.

He was a great guy, and on this Memorial Day, he is in heaven where he will celebrate with other veterans through eternity with our Lord and Savior, Jesus Christ.

> *John, we are going to miss you!*

> *Semper fi!*

Since the funeral is going to be in a few days, Sherrie and I decided for me to continue walking until I could get a flight out and to be there for four or five days during the funeral.

During the waiting for the flight arrangements, I had much time to pray for John, my mother-in-law, Sherrie, and all the family.

May 24, 2014

I am walking through downtown Hutchinson, Kansas, and lo and behold, I see a license plate for the Baltimore Ravens!

I stopped to talk to the family, and they are from the White Marsh area and recently moved to Kansas. We talked about Baltimore and our mission.

They said to tell all their friends in Baltimore. *Go ravens!*

They also confided that one of their children is a Steelers fan. I told them that I would be happy to pray for that child's rehabilitation!

On this Memorial Day, I ask you to think of all those who have given their lives in the service of our country.

John Costa is one who lost his life defending this country, because his illness was brought about partially by his exposure to asbestos while in the military. He was a retired navy chief and an incredibly proud navy veteran.

I also ask you to remember the father of the chaplain of this walk, Father Bill Kuchinsky. He raised a tremendous family along with his wife.

Please also I ask you to remember the fathers of Nancy Krebs and Bob Tarola, both of whom fought as marines on Iwo Jima.

These four are shining examples of why we should be so grateful.

John's funeral is going to be on Saturday, so I will be leaving Kansas on Wednesday and returning on Sunday to spend time with my family.

I got back from Santa Fe from my trip at about midnight. With the four-hour drive from the hotel, I did not start walking until noon, but the important thing was the number of people I met in Hutchinson who were already engaged in the debate of how to help solve the needs of children with emotional, behavioral, or developmental disabilities.

I met one person who is an educator. She was explaining that even in Kansas, the funding for such programs has been cut back this year.

Linda commented that with the reduction in the funding, the concern is that the severity of the cases that they are seeing in the schools is increasing but the funding is declining. I am seeing that same problem everywhere in the United States and probably in the world.

I had a peaceful time to think about John Costa, knowing that he is in a better place and is with God and the Blessed Mother in heaven.

Tomorrow after Mass, I will be heading out toward Route 61 North on my way up to Emporia.

May 25, 2014

I attended Mass at Saint Teresa of Avila Church in Hutchinson, Kansas. What a faithful community and unbelievably dedicated parish priest!

When I met the pastor before Mass, his first comment was, "Is there anything we can do to help?"

As I left Mass, without even asking, the first thing he did was to give me his blessing.

Thank you, Father, and thank you to the laity of the parish for your kindness.

Talk about gratitude!

I was walking on Route 61, and it just finished raining.

In the distance, about a half mile away, I saw a car pull off to the side of the road. The speed limit on that section of the highway was seventy miles per hour.

The car inched up to me, and the couple asked if I needed anything or if I needed a ride.

What was significant was that this delightful couple was willing to pick me up, turn around, and go back where they had just come from. It also could have meant that they saw me, passed me, turned around, and came back to offer me a ride. Whichever it was, they went really far out of their way to help a total stranger!

As I described the mission of the Good Shepherd Sisters to the couple, I could tell that they were touched. Their kindness motivated me, which made it easier to put one foot in front of the other to complete my journey.

You would be amazed at what impact you can have from a random act of kindness.

We completed twenty-five miles today in weather that was on and off between raining and sunshine.

This is the first time in the entire journey since March 15 that I had to wear my rain gear for most of the day. The gear held up well.

Tomorrow I am heading off to Newton and Emporia, Kansas.

Life Lessons Learned: Sincere compassion gives people in need hope.

May 26, 2014

> May 26, 2014 - Day #73 - Emporia, KS - 1490 miles down, 1316 left to go! 53.10% of the walk completed! — with Frank Ryan in Emporia, KS.

I received many touching comments from supporters while walking.

> *Tom, I cannot begin to thank you enough for your kindness and generosity to me and all of our veterans. Your support during this journey has been exceptional and made it that much easier. On those mornings when I was struggling to get up and get out of bed to get moving I thought of your kind words. You, Greg, Pam, and the entire MACPA Team have made this journey that I will never forget. I always knew while I was walking that you were there with me in spirit and prayer.*

While walking, I received many questions about the walk itself and what it was like since the persons asking were considering a walk themselves. In one response, I said,

> *I'm walking west to east. We have it published a route for number of reasons but predominately because I have to be flexible about the route changes due to traffic conditions. Is there a reason you're asking that I might be able to assist you with?*

> *When are you planning on doing it? Got a lot of recommendations of what I would do differently if I would do it over again.*

Unfortunately I don't know anything about you so answering that question is difficult. If you were in outstanding physical condition and have had a complete physical and cleared by doctors that's one thing but if you haven't done any training at all I would suggest you not do it. I somewhat trained my entire life for this. I'm a retired Marine but even with that I found that the training that I did not do in the four months before I left really affected the first month and a half of the walk. I just don't have enough information to go on to really advise you on this but I would caution you that this is not something you want to undertake if you're not prepared.

Life Lessons Learned: Give advice with thought, concern, and respect. Glib advice can do more damage than good.

It was a challenge getting twenty-five miles in today! I was beginning to realize that I was no longer twenty-one!

We just moved our base of operations to Emporia, and we were able to get all the way through Newton and Peabody today. There are some beautiful towns in Kansas. By tomorrow, I expect to get to Strong City and Emporia before I head out for the funeral.

In Newton and Peabody, I saw a contrast between the two cities that was fascinating.

Newton is a major rail hub and is thriving with only what appear to be minor issues relative to the downtown city area.

Peabody is a beautiful town with an entirely different story. It was a major Mennonite settlement back in the 1800s. It is a farming community with rail going through it. It seems to be suffering from population decline, as I have seen with so many small towns during this journey.

The scenes reminded me that the high cost of running companies and governments is causing a population shift from rural areas that may not be healthy for our nation in the long run.

The folks in Peabody were incredibly cordial. Everyone stopped to talk. One resident mentioned that he left Kansas City because he wanted to get out of the rat race, but now he feels he must move back because there are no jobs.

It reminded me that we have to be careful to be good stewards of the resources we have so that we do not inadvertently undermine our future.

Life Lessons Learned: **Stay relevant. Learn, grow, expand. Change is inevitable.**

May 27, 2014

A supporter asked me how the walk works with the support vehicle when I am by myself.

> *It depends upon the area . . . So what I do is I follow along the route and reposition the car as I'm walking which means in some cases I'm walking the same areas twice and some areas I'm not covering. I typically do that and 4 mile bursts. Hope that makes sense. :) we started doing it this way since I'm by myself and the safety in some areas became a major concern.*

To another supporter, I was answering her question about the progress so far:

> *The "bad" news is I had hoped to average 32 miles per day. :). Missed that dream on the first day of the trip! All that being said I'm very pleased with the progress so far. It only happened because of your encouragement,*

I had some interesting things happen again.

I bumped into a special-education teacher from Kansas who told me how important it is to take care of one child at a time and how important parental involvement is. She said that parental involvement is a key, along with strong educators and a motivated child.

We finished walking through Emporia, and I was amazed by how beautiful the city is. They have taken urban renewal to a new level. It gave me some ideas about perhaps ways we can use similar thoughts at Good Shepherd. Finding new and better ways of doing things while keeping the traditions that are tried and true seems to make sense to me.

Life Lessons Learned: **Learn from one another.**

Today, due to Diana Ellis's persistence, I am meeting with a fellow walker. Ian is walking for mental health issues.

Ian and I met in Yates Center, Kansas. We are kindred spirits of sorts. Ian is walking to raise awareness of mental health issues in honor of his brother Ryan. He is walking from east to west and started in Virginia Beach. I am walking across the United States for Good Shepherd Services and to raise awareness of the needs of children with emotional, behavioral, and developmental disabilities.

Our paths crossed today in Kansas, and we thought we would have a little reunion as we took a brief time out from our journey.

I wrote this to my friend Karl:

> *Karl actually our routes intersect because we are both going diagonal. Ian going from Virginia Beach to San Francisco and I went from San Diego to Ocean City so our routes intersected (in Kansas). We gave each other general pointers about what to avoid and what to look for.*

Kay asked me if I had lost weight while walking, and this was my response:

> *Kay I definitely recorded my weight when I started but I have no idea what I weigh now. I do know that my appetite is expanded exponentially. :). Just hope that that doesn't translate to my waistline!*

May 28, 2014

When I arrived at BWI, it was the first time I had been home to see Sherrie since we started our walk. Coming home to attend the funeral of her dad was a sad reminder of how fragile life is and how important it is for us to remember to care for one another and to pray.

I wrote this on the blog:

> *I ask you to keep him and all the other faithfully departed in your prayers this weekend.*

> *John was a retired Navy chief and after his retirement from the military he served over 20 years as a director of engineering for a hospital.*

> *What is remarkable about him though is that he came from an extremely difficult childhood that would have done in anyone else but not him. He was placed in a work farm at age 9 with his brother.*

Instead of it making him bitter he rose to the occasion, devoted his life to his family, and was faithful to our Savior at his death.

The caring and compassion that he showed for his children exemplified his life of devotion.

If you have a chance this weekend and your parents are still alive, please give them a call and tell them that you love them.

I said to a good friend of mine the other day that I would give up anything to be able to talk with my dad one more time for an hour. I remember this past Father's Day that I heard his voice for the first time that I ever remember when my nephew found a recording that was made of his voice during (or shortly after) World War II. For those of you that do not know, my father passed away when I was three.

So please use this occasion of remembering John Costa to contact your parents and just tell them that you love them.

Remember that in the next life all the faithful will be together again. What a wonderful thought.

I will be getting back to Kansas on Sunday and expect to be in Missouri by Wednesday morning. Just outside of Ottawa Kansas on my journey now.

And to Ian, safe travels my friend. You, your brother Ryan, and your parents were in my prayers today during my walk.

May 30, 2014

One of the questions that we received was from a perspective walker who was curious about safety. Anne Rochon brought up some interesting thoughts about planning for a walk of this magnitude.

I told Anne that in the western part of the United States, I carried and needed bear spray. I never used it, but it was very useful to have for some of the events that happened with animals, particularly wild abandoned dogs.

I carry both a backpack and a cart, but when I use the cart, I prefer to put the backpack in it so I am just pushing the cart. It was important to me to always carry the prayer petitions with me, because that was why I was walking. Very seldom during the walk did I not have them with me, and usually that was because I changed backpacks and forgot to move all the materials from the one backpack to the other.

The only place where the cart was a problem was in the New Mexico and Oklahoma and Texas areas, where the winds in the Mesa and the

Great Plains were horrific, which made using the cart too difficult. Other walkers I heard from felt that the cart was tremendous.

What I prefer to do when the winds are horrific is to stage gear for walking and carry as little gear as I can.

One very powerful piece of advice that I received from Greg Conderacci was to only take what you absolutely need. It was funny that I knew that from the Marine Corps but, for some reason, forgot it when I was planning this trip. Forgetting that powerful lesson is one of the reasons I developed some foot problems in the very beginning of the walk, because as I was walking down mountains, I had to simultaneously hold the cart back to keep it from getting away from me. The countermotion of going downhill while pulling a cart back created horrific friction on my feet.

May 31, 2014

The funeral services were a beautiful spiritual beginning to the next life in heaven with the Most Holy Trinity and the Blessed Mother of Jesus. The followers on the blog, the navy, the VFW, and the friends of the family provided such comfort for Sherrie and her mom and family.

I head back to Kansas City tomorrow and resume walking tomorrow as well.

I expect to be in Missouri by Tuesday evening or Wednesday morning.

Keep our mission of the Sisters of the Good Shepherd and Good Shepherd Services in your prayers.

June 1, 2014

It is all a matter of perspective!

I was at BWI airport, returning to Kansas, when I met Donna and Bill. My flight routed me through Orlando to Kansas.

Talk about two incredibly positive people. I was explaining to Bill, and he asked me why I was limping. I told him that my Achilles' heel was bothering me just a bit.

He then showed me his prosthetic device and explained to me about the impact of what happened when he had a motorcycle accident at age twenty-three when he was a New York City policeman.

The pleasant conversation and positive attitude of this potentially life-altering event gave me a new perspective on how to help our children.

It reminded me that there is always time for a new start. Either we can let life alter us or we can overcome obstacles.

Life Lessons Learned: **It is never too late to start over, to make a fresh start.**

I saw the same positive behavior in Greensburg, Kansas, and Bucklin, Kansas.

Shortly after I met Donna and Bill, I met a young couple building a great pyramid with a set of cards. It reminded me that every great program starts with one block at a time.

It's a matter of perspective. It's a matter of patience. It's a matter of persistence. Most importantly, it's a matter of faith.

Message from Elissa Fiore, a friend of Sherrie, about her dad:

> *Frank! I am so sorry to hear about Sherrie's father. I texted her not knowing about it but I had a sinking suspicion & Stevie confirmed . . . Also, are you still trekking through Kansas?*

The tremendous impact of caring from Elissa was such a comfort for Sherrie.

Powerful words impact powerful caring.

Life Lessons Learned: **Kind words can work miracles. Harsh words can destroy.**

June 2, 2014

There were lots going on today on the first day back on the walking trail.

We completed most of the trek through Ottawa and Olathe, Kansas, and got a little over twenty-five miles done. I was a little surprised that not walking for four days had an immediate impact on my walking endurance in that I had to pace it a little slower initially until I worked the "kinks" out of the muscles. This shows the impact of age on the human body.

One of the many highlights today was I stopped by on a special trip to Topeka to see my friends at the Kansas Society of CPAs. I was telling them how incredibly hospitable and friendly Kansans are.

I still have not yet had one bad experience on this entire journey. Every experience has been extremely positive.

Topeka is a beautiful capital as well.

I was walking by a Payday Loan sign. I find those types of loans very problematic, because they are so costly, and I remember those types of situations that affected my mom after my dad died.

The problem is that so many Americans are living one paycheck to the next such that these types of lenders flourish.

It reminded me that anytime we ask people to help us, we have to be good stewards of those resources that they provide us, because it may be all that they have.

Life Lessons Learned: **When we ask for help, we have to be good stewards of the gifts given to us.**

On the faith note, I have people tell me often that it is hard to have faith.

I was in Olathe. I was walking underneath a railroad bridge. A train came by, and I never once considered that the bridge would collapse on me. Every day we have faith in the roads that we travel and the bridges that we go over, so why would it be that much more difficult to believe and have faith in our Savior?

I am absolutely convinced and have faith that the solutions to our problems of helping children with behavioral, emotional, and developmental disabilities will come about. We just have to have faith.

We cross into Missouri late tomorrow. I am going from Olathe into Kansas City and then into Missouri.

June 3, 2014

Missouri is the "Show me" state.

June 3, 2014 - Day #81 - Grandview, MO - 1589 miles down, 1217 left to go! 56.63% of the walk completed! — with Frank Ryan.

I heard from my dear friend Skip Counselman, and I told him, "Skip I believe they should name a state after you. You have devoted so much time for worthwhile causes. It's been an absolute pleasure working with you and Margie! Still believe deep down you're really in the marines!"

We are under a tornado watch tonight. Please pray for those folks in Iowa and Nebraska who have been hit by the tornadoes this evening.

Despite the threat of weather, it was a wonderful day today, and we completed over twenty-seven miles.

I was a little surprised at the number of miles completed in light of the weather, or should I say the effects of the weather on people of my age!

June 4, 2014

I am in Grandview, Missouri, right now. I am just a little bit north of my route on Route 150 before I head into Warrenton.

I am still amazed that in my journey so far, I have not met one person who has had a negative reaction to what we are doing at Good Shepherd. We have a really good group of people in our nation. God bless you all.

We are walking along another rail line, and this one will follow the road I am on for a total of seven hundred miles.

"1589 is well past Halfway Colonel!" Getting this message really motivated me. Funny that when I had done twenty-six miles and only had 2,780 miles left to go, it was not as motivating! It is all a matter of perspective.

Talk about six degrees of separation!

I was in a parking lot and wearing a T-shirt from the Baltimore marathon from last year. (Incidentally, I walked the marathon. I did not run it!)

A gentleman came up to me and said he did not expect to meet someone from Baltimore in Missouri and that he was from Baltimore as well.

We talked for a while, and I explained the mission of the Good Shepherd Services and also about the walk across America. We also talked about Saint Agnes Hospital in Baltimore.

As soon as I mentioned those two issues, the names that we knew in common started the flow incessantly.

Jim Frederick was in Missouri on business and was with the firm of Goodell DeVries.

So from a personal perspective, just be careful anytime you are acting up, and do not be stunned if all of a sudden you find out that someone you have just met knows someone that you know.

I think it is called poetic justice!

Life Lessons Learned: **Always act with dignity. You never know who is watching. Our Savior is always with us, and so are many others.**

What a wonderful night!

Due to the passing of my father-in-law, I was unable to get to the wedding of my niece/cousin (we are actually cousins, but we have a very close family relationship, so I am more like her uncle and her mom, Jeanne-Marie, is more like my sister).

Since I am in the Missouri area and Amanda and Patrick are in Leavenworth with the army, we met for dinner.

We got a little over twenty-one miles, and it was a wonderful trip through Missouri.

We made it past Lee's Summit on my way to Warrensburg. I am not too far from Pittsville.

I stopped at Holy Spirit Catholic Church in Lee's Summit and had a wonderful discussion with the members of the parish staff.

The heel of my foot was acting up a little bit, so I went back to wearing the brace. I am feeling pretty good right now with the brace.

June 5, 2014

It was a great day for a walk!

It is the first full day of pouring-down rain. It turned out to be absolutely beautiful after the storm. I could do without the lightning and thunder though!

The tornado supercell seemed like it was forming near my walk route. I have never seen a tornado cell form, but I have heard the warnings this week. The winds kicked up, so I began to seek shelter just in case.

I am near Lone Jack, Missouri.

All clear! Winds were coming out of the east and then the west then downdrafts, and it dissipated almost as quickly as it started. There were a few knocked-over trees and branches. Of course, I also had to change clothes. This is the part of the trip where you have to be extremely careful about immersion foot.

With the change in weather, it turned out to be a fascinating day. I realize that I now look forward to the uncertainty in my life, which is not always a personal strong suit for me.

***Life Lessons Learned*: Uncertainty can be fun. Embrace it.**

Missouri is beautiful! I have been very impressed with the towns.

Lone Jack was interesting in that it was a site of a Civil War battle in 1862. For some reason, I did not remember that the Civil War battlefields went this far west.

The weather event today was fascinating as well. I had never seen anything like that, although the tornado never materialized. Thank God. I never have seen the winds change direction 180 degrees that rapidly, and the downdraft was dramatic as well.

I got my haircut in Warrensburg from some super guys who were more than happy to listen about the Good Shepherd mission.

June 6, 2014

Many wonderful things happened today. In fact, it was a miraculous day.

The day started in Warrensburg, where I met Jimmy D, who was driving a bus for a group of college students. Talk about an all-around good guy who was genuinely interested in our mission and very engaged in the concerns for young children. He made my day!

We were heading on Route 50 eastbound, and I got to the town of Knob Noster. I actually stayed on Route 50 and almost bypassed the town because it is off the main road.

For some reason, at the next exit off Route 50, I turned around and walked back into the town, and then I met George and Sandy. Both were tremendously spiritual people. We talked for about an hour about all the different issues of the various Christian faiths and our similarities and our differences. We talked about the need to unify our efforts for the common good of people.

From there, I continued eastbound, and I was heading toward Sedalia, Missouri. From the other side of the highway, a young couple stopped me and yelled across a four-lane highway if I needed any help or wanted a ride. I yelled back that I was walking across the United States, and the young gentleman came all the way across the four-lane divided highway to talk to me about our mission and Good Shepherd. He was a young father of four and told me that he decided to go back to church because of our walk.

We ended the day in Sedalia, and all was good!

By the way, we got twenty-eight miles in today—the best to date.

June 7, 2014

Interesting weather today!

The day started with a tremendous downpour with thunder and lightning. I went through two pairs of boots and two pairs of socks. By afternoon, the skies cleared with intermittent showers. All that means is that you are not sure how to dress!

We got twenty-five miles in, which I did not expect because changing clothes can sometimes interfere with walking, which I guess just means that these old bones are getting a little creaky! ☺

June 8, 2014

In Sedalia, I had to take care of some maintenance issues on the support vehicle and stopped by the Firestone Care Center. Cody and the entire team were so incredibly helpful.

After dropping the vehicle off, I went to Mass, which is always a source of comfort to me. The Mass is the manifestation of the Last Supper and, in my faith, the miracle of bread and wine being transformed into the body and blood of Christ.

We got twenty-five miles in, but it was a labor of love, I have to admit. My energy level started to drop off after about eighteen miles, and the last seven were an interesting evolution. I am surprised I was not pulled over by the police for impeding the flow of traffic.

I was so slow for the last seven miles that two turtles passed me. :)

We made it all the way to California, Missouri, and just a little bit past there on my way to Jefferson City.

I am into some rolling hills, which make the trip go by faster.

The change in scenery on the journey has been a rather pleasant one. When I needed it to be flat, it was flat, and when I needed some hills for diversity, it was there too.

> June 8, 2014 - Day #86 - California, MO - 1716 miles down, 1090 left to go! 61% of the walk completed!

June 9, 2014

Bill Sheridan, a friend of mine from the MACPA, asked me if we could possibly meet in Saint Louis. I mentioned to him, "Bill, I will be in Saint Louis on the fifteenth of this month. I would be there sooner, but I have a teaching assignment outside of the state on the twelfth and thirteenth."

Bill put out a notice to the state CPA societies of my walk route, and his kindness made it a wonderful reception at every one of the state societies that I stopped in to see. Thank you, Bill!

My friend Jim asked me a question about the route on the Bay Bridge in Maryland, and I told him, "Jim, you're not allowed to cross the bay bridge on foot. I'm just transporting to the other side by car and then making up the miles on the other side."

We had asked the state of Maryland for permission to walk across the Bay Bridge, but we were denied. What I did then was walk the five miles of the bridge as additional "makeup" miles on the other side of the bridge. I really wanted to walk the bridge, but I also understood the safety issues of the winds at that altitude as well as the traffic impact of me trying to do that.

We made it through Jefferson City today on Route 50. I am trying to stay as much as I possibly can on business Route 50 due to traffic and safety issues.

In the first two hours of walking, someone stopped to pray with me. I thought that was such a beautiful gesture. During that same two hours,

I met more people who were offering advice about how we can use our joint efforts to solve problems for children.

I am convinced that to impact our children in our care, we have to be willing to challenge the status quo.

I see it everywhere I go that change that is well thought out can have a very favorable effect on people. Jefferson City is a classic example in my mind of planning with a purpose. I see other areas that tried to hold on to the way things have been done before and they have failed in the process.

Life Lessons Learned: **Plan with a purpose in mind. Stay focused on the mission.**

Our core beliefs must remain unchanged, but the peripheral issues should be able to be changed based upon a well-thought-out plan.

Our faith is one of those core values that will serve us well as we attempt to implement crisis planning for dealing with those in need.

Brian conducted another interview today and asked me questions given to him from the children at Good Shepherd. The last question about why I was walking for them chocked me up so much that I could barely speak. All I wanted to tell them was that we all love them and that they can count on us. To think that just a month earlier I thought about stopping the walk, I became chocked up, because I thought that I almost let them down, but *we* continued the journey through the love of our Savior, the Blessed Mother, and his emissaries on earth—all of you and my dear friend Greg Conderacci.

June 10, 2014

The day started out perfect. We were expecting rain and missed it! We did get rain later in the day, but it's all good. It is all good regardless of the weather because of what happened today.

I was stunned by the unparalleled generosity, kindness, and caring of so many Missourians. I am not normally moved to being misty eyed, but this one did it.

First, I ran into Barry again this morning, who prayed with me again, and we had a wonderful conversation.

On the way to Linn, Missouri, I was stopped by a local sheriff. He said he was concerned about my limp and wanted to know if I needed a ride. I assumed he needed to see my ID card, and he said no but asked if I needed a ride. His genuine caring and concern were typical of the actions I have seen from so many wonderful law enforcement throughout this journey.

When I was walking through Union, I saw a statue of Benjamin Franklin. I thought it would be funny to take a selfie of me with this statute since Ben Franklin is from Pennsylvania as well.

Out of the blue, a young woman, Dawn, stopped and offered to take the picture of me with the statue. It was so incredibly kind, especially since she had to stop on a busy downtown street to do it. She told me about her son Vincent and other members of her family, and I told her about Good Shepherd.

Then I stopped at the hotel in Union for the night. At the front desk was one of the most delightful and helpful people I have ever meet. Her name is Vanessa. She referred me to a restaurant nearby.

When I got to the restaurant, the entire staff was so incredibly welcoming even though I got there only fifteen minutes before they were scheduled to close.

Trying to be respectful of the closing time and having been a waiter and a busboy myself before, I wanted to speed up eating. Jessica, Alex, and everyone were so cordial that they were not concerned about the closing time.

When I asked for my bill, I was told that it was taken care of. I told Jessica and Alex and others that they did not need to do that, and they said that they realized that. Using the Missouri and Kansas expression, I thought, let me "pay it forward."

The other couple eating and the entire staff then engaged in a very lengthy discussion with me. This overwhelming sense of generosity and caring that I have experienced has touched me when it is so easy for all of us to become cynical with life.

It reminded me of Bucklin, Kansas, when a similar thing happened. I was touched then and astonished now.

For all those young people who I am supposed to be mentoring, I want to offer my deepest gratitude for mentoring an old man that we have so much to be grateful for.

On a separate note, you should have seen the storm front today! My personal friendship experiences were so overwhelming that the weather front had no impact!

June 12, 2014

We made great progress today and are near Pacific, Missouri. Throughout the day, it was threatening rain, but I only got caught in the rain once.

I am heading to the airport to fly to Flathead, Montana, to work for three days. I have to keep reminding myself I have to pay for this hobby of mine! It is a labor of love!

I will be back walking in Saint Louis on Sunday and expect to meet the Sisters of the Good Shepherd then.

I hope you have an opportunity to meet these wonderful sisters who care about taking care of the most abandoned souls—one child at a time.

They are truly my heroes.

June 13, 2014

I flew out of Indianapolis airport to Flathead Lake in Kalispell, Montana.

I was playing with a black lab at Flathead Lake, and I saw something in that black lab that many people forget: enthusiasm!

The enthusiasm that this puppy had for playing and pleasing was so wonderful to see. A youngster, an infant, frequently has that same type of enthusiasm for life.

Most people have that enthusiasm for life until we sometimes let life get the better of us.

Life Lessons Learned: **Do not let life take your enthusiasm. Find an energy buddy and keep your enthusiasm intact.**

If we maintain our enthusiasm and optimism and Christ-centered life, then that enthusiasm and optimism remain whole. If we let cynicism take hold, that cynicism can overwhelm us. Being cynical in no way helps us to be able to solve this problem of emotional, behavioral, and developmental disabilities in children. Try watching a little puppy and see if you can restore your own optimism and enthusiasm for life.

We were walking through Big Fork, Montana, to pray and think about our children, when a car stopped me and asked if I knew who owned a particular house.

I told the two delightful people that I was not from the area, and we started talking about the walk across America. I told them that it was for children with emotional, behavioral, and developmental disabilities. They then told me that they were with Special Olympics of Montana.

Well, that started a lively discussion. They got out of the car and took pictures, and we had a wonderful conversation.

It is again the hand of God that is at work.

I saw this attitude of enthusiasm from these two young folks that I met in Montana. What spontaneity and love of children. Enthusiasm is infectious!

One of the lessons I have learned during this walk is that every day, I saw challenges and adventures. It just motivated me to see what is just over the top of the next hill. I was almost eager with anticipation regardless of how tired I might have felt.

Also, as I was walking today, I was thinking about forgiveness.

I have mentioned to many people that this walk is a walk of atonement and gratitude.

Life Lessons Learned: If you have hurt someone, ask for forgiveness.

For the walk of atonement, I have asked anyone that I have hurt to forgive me, people that I have disappointed to pray for me, or people that I have helped to help another.

In the spirit of the idea of forgiveness that our Savior provides for us, think about the comfort that forgiveness provides us in knowing that regardless of what we have done, he forgives us. I hope that is as comforting to you as it is for me.

I hope this weekend, Father's Day, we, as children, will take time out to talk to our parents and try to remember all the good that they have done rather than the problems that have happened in our lives.

Unfortunately, parenthood is frequently an on-the-job training. Sometimes what we learn with the first few children is modified or relaxed or strengthened as we have more children.

Sometimes we do not learn it until it is too late and our children are grown. As grandparents, then perhaps we can help remove the pain of problems caused when we were parents ourselves.

True peace comes when we learn to forgive, not when we hold grudges.

I told my friends on Facebook that

> *I hope you use this weekend as an opportunity to extend forgiveness to someone you have been harboring concerns about for a long time.*
>
> *I pray that tranquility of the pictures will help give you the tranquility of peace to forgive and seek forgiveness.*
>
> *I pray every day that I become the type of person that my dogs think I am!* ☺

June 14, 2014

From Rick Stanley: "You're not alone."

That wonderful comment from Rick came at just the right time. We are never alone—not with our Savior nor with our friends. Thank you, Rick, for this great reminder!

What a wonderful experience yesterday.

Sr. Mary Catherine of the Sisters of the Good Shepherd sent me this note in anticipation of our get-together in Saint Louis. I think I can finally see the end even though I have so far to go.

> *Hi, Frank, You are amazing! What a courageous journey! Thanks for keeping us informed. I am wondering how you will get to St. Louis tomorrow!*
>
> *You are in my/our thoughts and prayers, Sr. Mary Catherine.*

We are back on the walking trail! We got back from Montana and start back up again tomorrow morning. We are now less than one thousand miles to go!

I jokingly told everyone that I can smell the Atlantic Ocean from here.

Well, my walk may be on hold for just a little bit. On my return from Montana, the airline lost my luggage. Since I was walking, I had to stay put since they were not willing to deliver the luggage to where I was walking.

At first, I was pretty upset because I had a schedule. Little did I know that I needed to remember once more that it is not my schedule but the schedule of our Savior. Just hours later, I would meet people that I would not have met had it not been for this delay.

It is amazing the number of times that I needed to learn this lesson. All happens for a reason, and the fact that I do not know what it is, is absolutely unimportant!

***Life Lessons Learned*: Look at inconveniences and setbacks with grace, dignity, and enthusiasm.**

June 15, 2014

The hand of God is alive and well again.

While I was waiting for my gear to be found by Delta Airlines, I stayed around Indianapolis for the night.

I went to Mass today at Saint Paul the Apostle Catholic Church. The pastor is Father Darvin Winters. In his sermon, Father Winters mentioned a priest by the name of Msgr. Satterfield. I knew a Msgr. Satterfield at Mount Saint Mary's College.

After Mass, I asked Father Winters if he was a Mountie. He smiled and said yes. I told him that Msgr. Satterfield had previously been my parish priest.

It was like old home week. It was a wonderful Father's Day present in addition to the messages I received from my children and my daughter-in-law.

I ask you to keep Father Winters in your prayers, because he has just been accepted for active duty United States Air Force as a chaplain.

He will be Major Winters here very shortly! ☺

To all the fathers today, happy Father's Day!

Just found my equipment! I am back on the road again!

Thank you, Delta agents!

I just had one of the best days of my life!

We arrived at the Sisters of the Good Shepherd house in Saint Louis and saw the wonderful sisters who have devoted their lives to our Savior, our Blessed Mother, and our children.

I had an incredibly wonderful time. Thank you so much!

June 15, 2014 - Day #93 - St. Louis, MO - 1833 miles down, 973 left to go! 65% of the walk completed! — with Frank Ryan.

June 16, 2014

The Sisters of the Good Shepherd posted this message:

> *Frank Ryan has been walking across America for Good Shepherd Services, Baltimore, since March 15. Frank passed through St. Louis Sunday evening and stopped at the Province Center for a quick visit with the Sisters. He had dinner with the community, chatted with the Sisters at Immaculate Heart and completed a video interview with our communications coordinator. Frank heads out Monday morning to continue his walk across America.*

From Kay King:

> *Are you in Illinois now?*

From Maggie Esselman:

> *Frank, you have been an inspiration to me since the first time I met you. You continue to amaze me. My prayers are with you every day, every step of the way. If anyone can accomplish this, you can do it. God bless you, every step of the way.*

Response to Kay King:

> *I still have about 15 more miles to do before I cross the Mississippi River. :)*

To Dave, I responded:

> *Dave I haven't crossed the Mississippi yet. Hope to do that in about four hours.*

We had many fascinating things happen today. I never cease to be amazed at the hand of God in everything that has happened on this walk.

First, I was going to visit with the Delta Sigma Theta sorority. I met with the East Saint Louis chapter of some of the most remarkable women you can possibly imagine.

You should see the phenomenal work that these women are doing to help children in East Saint Louis.

I also had the opportunity to meet the mayor of East Saint Louis along with the delightful chance to see three of the Sisters of the Good Shepherd as well.

The Deltas are very big in child-related issues, particularly mental health, medical, and education.

Thank you so much, Adriann and all the Sisters of the East Saint Louis chapter of the Deltas.

I crossed into Illinois by crossing the Eads Bridge over the Mississippi River.

Unfortunately, there was not a welcome sign that I could take a photograph of because I was in the middle of the bridge and the state line is in the middle of the river.

On this walk across the bridge, I met Julie, who was the second person during this trip to ask if she could pray with me. Her prayer was so heartfelt it motivated me for the rest of the day.

God bless you, Julie!

The Mississippi River was awe-inspiring. I could have stood on that bridge for hours, watching the river and the buzz of cargo moving around the busy river area.

During my last day in Missouri, I also had a chance to stop by the Missouri Society of CPAs.

I felt so welcome. It was another chance to meet fellow CPAs.

I also had the opportunity to see a fellow instructor, Mike Morgan, at the Missouri Society of CPAs.

June 17, 2014

Just as I think I have had the best day of the trip, another one comes along.

You cannot possibly tell me that this country does not have great people in it.

I am more convinced than ever that with the collective goodwill and efforts of so many great Americans, we can make a real positive impact on the needs of children with emotional, behavioral, and developmental disabilities.

Yesterday's great day with the Deltas was unbelievable.

Today I got into Highland, Illinois, and a very touching and compassionate thing happened.

I was stopping for the evening even though I still had seven more miles to go on my journey, when I met Lorie, who is the general manager of the Holiday Inn Express in Highland.

I asked her if there was a Laundromat close by, and she said that they would be happy to do it for me, which I said was not necessary. Lorie was so willing to help, and at that point, I said that I was so tired, that I was thankful for her offer to help.

Life Lessons Learned: **Accept help gracefully and gratefully. Be thankful.**

She mentioned that there would be no cost. I thought she was referring to the laundry. Instead she had decided to comp the room for the evening.

I was stunned by her generosity and mentioned that I would be making a contribution to Good Shepherd Services on their behalf for her generosity. I said it was important to me that every dollar raised go to the children. You could tell that Lorie was very moved by the mission of the sisters.

In Collinsville and Troy, Illinois, today, I had two wonderful experiences in which people, total strangers, stopped and offered to give me a ride and help me out.

One person even turned around to help me.

Both persons said they were concerned that it was so extremely hot, and with the high humidity, they wanted to do what they could do help.

This day is paralleling the day I had the day before. It is amazing how helpful people have been.

June 18, 2014

I started out walking today in Highland, Illinois.

As I started walking, I was passed by a young lady who was moving so quickly that I thought that I was standing still. Her speed impressed me.

As she turned around and started to pass me again, she asked me why I was walking with a backpack. I explained the walk and at the same time told her I was thankful she was not my commanding general in the Marine Corps, because I didn't think I could keep up with her.

Her name was Dee, and we had a pleasant conversation about Good Shepherd and our young children.

Not more than thirty minutes later, a car pulled over and the driver said, "Good morning, Colonel."

I knew it had to be Dee's husband, Mike!

When you do something like this, you cannot possibly imagine what it does for a person's morale. The gesture gave me that additional spurt of energy, which I really needed at this stage of the game.

The meeting with Dee and Mike, orchestrated by God, led Dee to call Bill Napper, who came out to see me. Bill is an editor of a newspaper he founded. Bill is also a retired US Marine!

It turned out Bill and I served in some of the same places.

It was a day to regale about our lives as Christians and as United States Marines. It just does not get any better than that!

Incidentally, there is a town in Illinois near Highland called Marine.

From Highland, I walked to Pierron, Illinois.

I stopped to ask if I could park the support vehicle near one of the local bars and received a beautiful welcome from the hostess and others in the establishment. In fact, Barbara even signed up to like the Good Shepherd Services Facebook page.

Also two young men, Patrick and Adam, stopped and asked me if I needed water. Help comes in every age, and help comes with compassion.

I ended the day outside of Greenville, Illinois, and I am now on my way to Vandalia.

Toward the end of the day, after I passed the US prison in Greenville, I ran into some people who were biking across the United States. They were doing it in twelve days, averaging 250 miles a day! They were heading toward Annapolis, Maryland. I prayed for them as they made their journey.

During my journey, I met many road warriors who were supporting wonderful missions, such as Good Shepherd. It was so heartwarming to know that so many folks care about others.

At the prison, there was a No Trespassing sign. Really? For some reason, I started laughing, saying that they probably did not have a huge problem with folks trespassing to get *in* to the prison—out of there, *yes*, but in? Really?

I had a wonderful dinner with Bill and Maureen Napper this evening.

I have been so honored to have dinner with them and have been so touched by their spirituality. Bill and I had a chance to reminisce about the Marine Corps. I was explaining to Bill and Maureen that Bill's coming into my life had significant effect on me.

When I was in Santa Rosa, New Mexico, I mentioned that I had a transformation in my prayers.

Prior to Santa Rosa, I would pray for something specific such as heat to dissipate, weather, and things like that.

After experiencing fifty-mile-an-hour winds with seventy-mile-per-hour gusts from Moriarty to Santa Rosa, it finally dawned on me that I should be praying instead for the ability to endure what Christ has put in front of me.

While I felt better about such a prayer, I felt that perhaps I was still not getting it.

Today Bill said something that caused me to realize that instead of praying just to endure, I should pray to accept whatever our Savior has for me and have faith that he will give me that which I can handle.

Have faith! The Sisters of the Good Shepherd have always reminded me to have faith, and I was able to experience that today through Bill.

Life Lessons Learned: **Have faith—faith to accept, endure, persevere, and be thankful.**

It started with Mike in California, Paul and Rosie, a young waitress in Bucklin, the Deltas, the entire Good Shepherd team, and so many others who have had such a huge influence on me.

I received a wonderful message from a person that I had met the day before. Barbara's comment was so touching, and little did she know that it was me who realized I met a wonderful person when I met her. She, and others, touched my life in such great ways. The power of human caring and compassion will solve so many problems.

Life Lessons Learned: **Caring and compassion for one another cure many ills.**

I recalled, outside of Dalhart, Texas, that a traveler told me that he was going to "hop" a train and I told him that was dangerous. He then said, "Who would care?" I told him I would. His eyes teared up. He stopped what he was about to do and started walking instead. God always provides inspiration for us to move on.

Later in the day, my daughter Kate sent me two pictures of my grandchildren, Nathan and Becca. I miss them so much, and getting the pictures so unexpectedly let me know that she cares. I do love them so.

June 19, 2014

I am overwhelmed at everyone's kindness.

I had two folks stop and offer me water within five minutes of starting out this morning.

My faith in humanity has been restored. Actually, it was my faith in my humanity in which I had to recognize that it was my responsibility to lead a Christ-like life. The cynicism that I had developed was my problem, and this walk was convincing me that it was me that had the problem.

After the early-morning hike, I stopped for breakfast, and a media person from the Bikers across America came over to talk. He was very emotional about what the Sisters of the Good Shepherd are doing to help children and about the walk.

With his comments in the restaurant, it caused quite a discussion at the Huddle House Restaurant.

That stop generated much discussion with many, many prayer requests.

Then when I was walking, Mike and Dee from Highland called just to make sure I was okay.

The walk today took me from Vandalia to Altamont.

I saw where Abraham Lincoln was a state senator in Illinois back in the 1830s. In seeing what Abraham Lincoln fought for, what he had a vision for, his faith in freedom and liberty for all was so apparent.

I could not help but think that the foundress of the Sisters of the Good Shepherd fought the same type of battles for young women.

In thinking of our mission to help children, it was pretty apparent to me that we have to have a vision to do that which we know is right regardless of how difficult it may be to do.

We need to create solutions for our children that are faith-based, meaningful, and can withstand academic rigor to ensure that we protect children in our care. It is important to me that this care be independent of federal or state funding so that it can be consistently applied for all families in need. Many people expressed concern that the task appeared overwhelming, and then I thought about what must have happened with Abraham Lincoln and Saint Mary Euphrasia, and I said, "Bring it on!"

I have no doubt that our mission is critical for children.

Life Lessons Learned: **All great change faces obstacles. Going against the status quo requires strength of conviction and fortitude.**

June 20, 2014

The temperature for the past few days has been in the midnineties with extremely high humidity. I experienced similar weather before, but I am almost into the hundredth day of the walk and the cumulative effects on my body are different than earlier on. Fatigue is different than just tired because of the duration of the walk.

As I was walking, a gentleman ran out from Al's Tires to give me some ice-cold water. My water had gotten pretty warm from the heat, and the cold bottle of water hit the spot. He was such an angel!

I see now that I have trained consistently to work in spurts, such as thirty or forty-five days, but this is not a sprint; it is a marathon, very much like caring for our children. Our care is a marathon and not a sprint, so the solutions are different. I need to remember this very valuable lesson!

Life Lessons Learned: **Fatigue is different than being tired. To go the distance, one must overcome fatigue. Train for the long run. Tired is only a state of mind and must be pushed through.**

It was about eleven miles into the day when my energy just died. I could barely move.

I started to get frustrated, but then I decided to pray and check my e-mail, because of course, when you are exhausted, one must check e-mail! By the way, I understand that is an unusual combination of things to do, to pray and check e-mail, but you are going to have to get over that! ☺

I received a message on Facebook from Mike, who is friends with Bill and Maureen and Dee and Mike in Highland.

Mike sent me a prayer that they said in his church group. The prayer literally lifted me up, and I started walking again.

I said to Mike,

> *Mike I really needed this today. About an hour ago I just plain ran out of energy. I am at 11 miles and was praying for inspiration help me go on. You did it my friend!*
>
> *I'm not sure if you all know how you came through today for me during my walk!*
>
> *Your prayers and your well wishes and ask of kindness had a tremendous effect on this old body.*

As I was walking into Effingham, Illinois, the first major buildings that I saw were Sacred Heart Parish.

I asked the church office if I could park my support vehicle there while I walked later in the day, and they were incredibly cordial and helpful. Father even blessed my prayer petitions.

I went to confession and Mass there on Saturday.

Sacred Heart of Jesus is the name of my parish in Cornwall, Pennsylvania. My pastor is a wonderful pastor.

I ended the day east of Montrose, Illinois, and all is well.

For all who helped this old man today, thank you!

June 21, 2014

Today was a light walking day—just fifteen miles.

I am east of Montrose, Illinois, and will be hitting the two-thousand-mile mark tomorrow, God willing.

I decided to do fewer miles today so that I could spend some time going to confession and going to Mass, which give me a chance to pray for those people who have been praying for me. The lesson about the marathon versus sprint also began to hit home. I realized that my walking, while not a sprint, would not be sustainable if I did not care for the physical stamina of the long-term effects of the walking.

As I was going to confession, I thought of many of my non-Catholic friends who talk about confession and do not appreciate the value of going to confession. I recognize that every time I sin, I have hurt someone else as well as hurt my relationship with God. One of the many problems with sin is that it makes it easier to do it again.

By discussing sin with the priest, you have a spiritual understanding and the rebuilding of that relationship with Christ because of the sin. It is a wonderful way of cleansing the soul and the mind so that you can remove all obstacles to the total union with Christ that comes when you have been saved.

I mentioned to you previously that a young man by the name of Joe at Al's Tire came running out to give me a bottle of cold water. I needed that ice-cold water!

Today I wanted to take my support vehicle to Al's just to have them check the tires, and when I got to about an eighth of a mile from their entrance, my tire went flat! If that had happened miles earlier, we would really have had a major problem. Am I feeling protected or what?

Mark and the entire staff did a tremendous job and had me turned around in no time. I see the hand of God at work here!

Have faith. My journey is never alone. It is why I say *we* all the time. My Blessed Mother Mary is with me, as is our Savior and all my friends—particularly Greg!

Life Lessons Learned: **We are never alone.**

June 22, 2014

I have had the chance to reflect quite a bit today. I remembered the so many unbelievably wonderful experiences on this trip that now I do not remember any of the discomfort.

I wondered if that is what heaven is like?

> *Another wonderful day! I think but I'm not hundred percent positive that we crossed over 2000 miles today. I'm going to ask Diana Ellis from Good Shepherd to confirm.*

We went from Greenup to Casey to just outside of Marshall, Illinois. So far, in two thousand miles and since March 15, 2014, I have met only positive people! Illinois has kept up the trend!

With that kind of attitude in this nation, I am positive we can make a major difference in the lives of our young children.

God willing, I expect to cross into Indiana tomorrow.

I promised Diana I would get a Welcome to Illinois sign as well as a Welcome to Indiana picture tomorrow! ☺

I was not able to get a Welcome to Illinois sign because of where they were located when I crossed the Mississippi River.

In Greenup, I also saw the world's largest chimes! Alice asked me a question about the chimes. "I wanted to Alice but there was no wind at all when I went by. I've seen them but I didn't hear them," I responded to the question about the wind chimes.

June 23, 2014

> *Yesterday was day #100 of the Walk Across America . . .*
> *Frank officially crossed over 2,000 miles! Congrats Frank!*

We visited Greenup, Illinois, today, the City of Porches. Greenup is very close to Lincoln's log cabin. It was, like so many towns that I have gone through, a beautiful community with great people.

> *Well we did it!*
> *We just crossed into Indiana!*
> *Thank you all so much for your support and prayers.*

We crossed into Indiana and the Wabash River, and when I crossed the river, the rain started coming down in buckets. I was drenched!

I also think I just had my first bad experience of the trip.

I was checking into a hotel in Terra Haute, and a young man, about fourteen years old, told me that his merit badge for the Boy Scout is to help elderly people. He said his granddad understood and explained to him how hard it is for people my age. ☺

I think I'm going to bed! ☺

We are ending the day in Terre Haute, Indiana.

I stopped for lunch at an IHOP. There was a delightful couple, Randy and Marsha, sitting near me, and we started up a conversation.

It turned out that he has thirteen grandchildren so far. He has suffered from some health issues, though, and I wanted to try to do something nice for him and take care of his meal. But before I could do that, he had taken care of mine, unbeknownst to me.

I was so taken aback by his kindness and generosity, particularly in light of what he has been through, that my family and I made a personal donation in Randy's and Marsha's names to Good Shepherd Services.

Randy, you really taught me something today. Thank you so much.

Life Lessons Learned: Be generous with others. Share what you have.

> June 23, 2014 - Day #101 - Terre Haute, IN - 2026 miles down, 780 left to go! 72% of the walk completed! — with Frank Ryan.

June 24, 2014

I was checking my Facebook message from a sixty-year-old who was planning on running across the United States in forty-six days or less.

So he, at age sixty, plans on running across America in forty-six days! Ouch! ☺ I was feeling sorry for myself for limping across the country in three times as long. Back to the drawing board on this old body of mine!

> *We just received my first emergency alert on my Weather system. It startled me to say the least. When severe storms are approaching, walking at 2.5 miles per hour is not a consoling thought.*
>
> *The previous warnings of severe thunderstorms and lightning have been in effect for three hours but flash flood warnings just issued for where I am.*
>
> *If you are in the affected areas please be safe.*
>
> *We also just received a tornado alert.*
>
> *One touched down about 20 miles from where I am.*
>
> *I am completely safe. I ask you to keep everyone in the tornado's path in your prayers.*
>
> *A large tornado touched down near Indianapolis and is moving just north of the city.*
>
> *Weather alerts coming out almost by the minute. The towns of Speedway and Flackville and Brooklyn Heights near Indianapolis are in the immediate path of the tornado.*
>
> *I am west of the tornado but in severe thunderstorms and lightning.*
>
> *Again I am safe but please pray for the people in the path of this tornado.*

My thoughts raced to my dear friend Karl Ahlrichs, who lives in the area of the tornado. I sent him a message:

Karl are you and your family okay! I have been praying for you my friend.

We are back on the road again. The skies are still dark, and I decided to take back roads to avoid traffic.

So many miles to go, places to see, and people to meet! :)

I ran into some things I just did not expect to run into.

We started the day east of Terre Haute and ended up just west of Greencastle on Route 40. I am staying in a hotel in Cloverdale, and at dinner tonight, I met a delightful family that included two national guardsmen, one of whom just returned from overseas and a brand-new three-week-old baby!

June 25, 2014

During my journey, I always welcomed e-mails and questions about the walk. One such question that I received was concerning my diet. I responded to John by saying,

> *John you should see how much I'm eating! I just know that*
> *when I stop walking I better slow down or I will weigh*
> *800 pounds.*

I made that comment to someone in jest but also very seriously. I was surprised that I was in a continuous feeding mode just in order to maintain my weight and my strength. Literally, I eat from sunup until sundown. I never count calories, but I eat for fuel. I learned quickly that the wrong diet could wreak havoc on my body.

Diet and the problems that many of our children have with childhood obesity caused me to think that perhaps the food aspects of our treatment plan must also be well researched and well thought out. Such diets are part of the treatment plan at Good Shepherd, and I thought that more research might be helpful.

There was also a fantastic post from a friend of mine who said, "Wow almost done!"

I still have 735 miles to go, and I do not feel like I am almost done. Seriously, that comment made me think about perspective, because in reality, I was almost done. The journey has come a long way, but the daunting task of walking 735 more miles was also very real.

The well-wishes have been a tremendous motivator. It made the isolation of being on the walk "alone" very tolerable.

We made it from outside of Greencastle to a few miles inside of the Marion County line, which is very close to Indianapolis.

Plainfield is a beautiful city. I did not realize the influence of the Friends Community in Plainfield. You should visit if you have the opportunity.

One thing that surprised me was when I took my shoe off and one more of my toenails fell off. I never realized when I started this walk that I would lose all my toenails. Yet every person I talked to who was a runner or bicyclist asked me how long it took me to lose my toenails. For some reason, I never thought that would be an issue. It was never uncomfortable, but I was surprised that it happened.

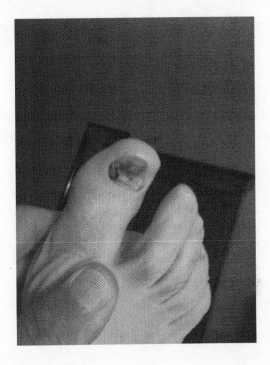

June 26, 2014

There were a number of comments on the blog about the compression pants that I was wearing. Obviously, all my marine friends, to include Sergeant Major Eddie Neas and Colonel John Buttil, could not resist giving me a hard time. I told them both,

I thought wearing Marine green with compression pants was an oxymoron. Didn't want to embarrass the Corps!!! :)

Both Sergeant Major Neas and Colonel John Buttil are my heroes.

My sergeant major is a Vietnam veteran and combat-wounded marine. But he was also willing to challenge the status quo, which he and I both did when we were in the civil affairs group.

Col. John Buttil challenged the status quo as well when he took the first deployment to Bosnia. I could always count on John's intellect and presence of mind in difficult situations. He was my executive officer, and I was extremely proud of him and his service.

That being said, both of them earned the right to give me a hard time, and they did it so well. They both need to remember, however, that payback is swift. ☺

Seriously though, those compression pants were unbelievably effective even though I looked horrible! My dear friend Father Bill Kuchinsky, our chaplain for the walk, even commented that I lacked fashion sense.

We got a late start walking today because I had an audit committee meeting by phone for one of the boards that I am on. We were able to start walking at 10:00 AM. It was all good!

We walked through Indianapolis. What a beautiful city.

The best part, though, was when I stopped by the Indiana Society of CPAs and saw some of my good friends. I have been doing lectures with the Indiana Society of CPAs for almost thirty years now. They are a great group of CPAs, and I enjoyed seeing them.

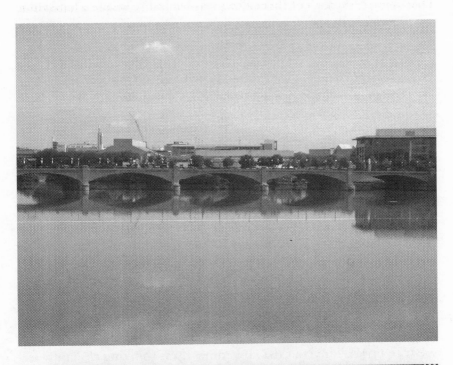

Due to a scheduling conflict since I was behind schedule compared to my original walk plan, Karl and I were not able to connect, and he sent me a message to which I responded:

> *Karl I know you were there in spirit. Your support during this entire journey has been remarkable and helpful. Your friendship means an awful lot to me. Thank you so much.*

> June 26, 2014 - Day #104 - Indianapolis, IN - 2090 miles down, 716 left to go! 74% of the walk completed!

When I saw the posting of the miles that we completed, the realization was beginning to hit me that soon I will complete the walk. We have come a long way, and we must now be prepared to go the distance—for our children, that is.

June 27, 2014

As I was walking, I was thinking of some of the expressions we parents use with our children. At the same time, I was thinking about my feet and some comments that I was talking to my brother about. I lost a couple of toenails this week from stubbing my toes!

My brother Bob just completed, at age sixty-seven, a volunteer fireman's course, and he graduated first in his class at age sixty-seven with well over thirty years of age difference between him and the other people who were in the program. He was then asking me about the walk and how my feet were holding up.

We both said we would never do it again for either his course or my walk, but we were extraordinarily happy that we have both done it.

This then gets back to the comments that parents make and how it affects what we do. I remember being told not walk with my head down. I was told to look straight ahead, stand tall, and be firm. All great advice but . . .

Following that advice when walking in uncharted areas, either a fireman's training course or walking across America, can get you seriously hurt.

I tell people I am only one sidewalk or hole in the road away from a broken ankle. It almost happened when I was in New Mexico.

At the same time, if you look down all the time to avoid falling, you miss so many beautiful scenes around you.

Life Lessons Learned: **Avoiding failure is not the measure of success.**

It's about risk and reward. It's about living life to the fullest or living life trying to avoid failure. Avoiding failure is not living life. It's nothing more than avoiding failure.

So when we look at creating a viable means of solving the problem of how to help children with emotional, behavioral, or developmental disabilities, we have got to be prepared to fail.

Part of the walk is the walk of atonement, because I failed.

You cannot let the fear of failure get in the way of our helping children and solving problems.

Life Lessons Learned: **The fear of failure kills more initiative than failure itself.**

I ask all of you to consider what you would do with your life if failure were not a possibility. Let yourself go, risk failing, make a difference!

I explained to the significant increase of new likes to the Facebook page some of the logistics of the walk so that some of the posts would make sense. I said,

> *For those that are new to the website I planned to walk across America full time from March 15 to July 1.*
>
> *If I wasn't done by July 1 I'll be doing it on a part-time basis about 3 to 4 days a week until I get done. That's the reason I started on the West Coast so if I did not get done by July 1 I could finish it up on weekends without incurring a lot of time lost trying to get back to the West Coast.*

So today, I drove back to my home office near York, PA and got my clothes and gear ready to start back to work directly from my walk across America on July 1.

The pictures are from York PA where I had my car serviced.

Right now I am returning to an area just east of Indianapolis to continue walking through July 1. I'm hoping to do 75 miles in the next three days.

I'm about 20 miles east of Indianapolis when I left to get my clothes and equipment.

A revised date to complete the walk across America is now towards the later part of August.

If things go normally once I start back to work on July 2, I could be done as early as August 15th.

Having to go back to work is a little bit of a challenge since I am beginning to enjoy this walk and all the great people that I am meeting. Since I am behind schedule, though, the logistics of getting materials prepared, licenses renewed, taxes done were becoming all too real. For instance, my inspection sticker on the car was due to expire on June 30, so I had to get it done.

But then I remembered this is a walk of gratitude, and every one of these issues I just mentioned is completely insignificant. It meant absolutely nothing in the grand scheme of things compared to the need for helping our children. I wondered how often I have wasted so much effort worrying about things outside of my control.

***Life Lessons Learned*: Do not let details overwhelm you or your plans.**

It is all a matter of perspective, and we have so much to be grateful for. This walk has been a life-altering event, and I will never forget the atonement and gratitude that is so essential for me to atone for the mistakes that I have made and give thanks for the gifts that Christ has given.

June 28, 2014

It is a little after 10:00 PM, and we just got done twenty-five miles in Indiana. We finished the day in Knightstown.

Today was overwhelming. I met so many people and had the opportunity to talk about the mission of Good Shepherd—from the parish priest at Saint Michael's to a homeless person I met outside of Greenfield to a state trooper on the SWAT team to a truck driver and his significant other and two high school students and an entire mental health awareness get-together in Greenfield.

On top of that, I met a navy veteran and his family at a restaurant in Greenfield.

Finally, in Knightstown I met two attorneys—one who worked with mental health and one who was a public defender—and their openness, candor, and compassion were touching.

The towns were pretty nice too!

All's well!

"Lenora thank you for making me feel so welcome," I responded to Lenora Keegan's comment.

June 29, 2014

Every day gets better than the last!

We started the day in Straughn, Indiana. From there we went through a number of absolutely beautiful towns that were reminiscent of the 1940s, '50s, and '60s in terms of the heritage of the area.

Some of the towns, such as Dublin, Cambridge City, Centerville, and East Germantown, were beautifully kept up in the heritage of the national historic road.

Just outside of Centerville, I had the chance to speak with an Indiana State policeman. He asked me if I had had any difficulty with being stopped along the way. I said absolutely not, and in fact, I found the police and the sheriffs to be incredibly helpful.

I also told him that one of the reasons I wanted to do the walk was because I was becoming cynical.

I mentioned to him that when you see the news, when you serve in Afghanistan and Iraq, when you see violence in many cities, you think that that is the norm rather than the exception.

I told him the walk was a walk of atonement and gratitude, and what I am most grateful for with this walk now is that I am no longer cynical.

We have a nation of really good people. I remember talking with Bill Napper about that as well. Bill's paper prints only good news.

This does not mean that we want people to bury their head in the sand about problems. What we want to do is put problems in perspective, or we risk becoming overwhelmed by the sheer magnitude of the bad news that is reported.

Accentuate the positive, as my good friend Jennifer Elder would say, rather than always reinforcing the negative.

Life Lessons Learned: Accentuate the positive. Be an energy buddy, not an energy thief.

At the end of the conversation, the police officer said he was thinking about perhaps taking a walk himself.

June 30, 2014

Well, we did it! We just crossed into Ohio.

To all the people I met in Indiana, thank you for your hospitality, compassion, and friendship!

To my good friend Johnny Baijan, happy birthday tomorrow, my friend. Johnny was my interpreter and a dear friend when we were together in Iraq in 2004 and 2005.

To Sister Claire Marie, I wanted to let her know that their dedication to our Savior and our Blessed Mother is what is amazing. I am merely grateful to be able to do this walk and to raise awareness. To her I said, "Sister, thank you so much for the prayers. You all are the ones who are amazing."

Father Bill as I get closer to when I'm going to West Virginia I'd love to coordinate with you to see you at least for a little bit and buy you lunch.

Priests and sisters are wonderful at deflecting kind words. They always return it to the sender. Now it is my turn to do that. The clergy are God's emissaries on this earth for which we should always be so thankful for these selfless servants.

God bless each and every one of them.

July 1, 2014

I am working at the Maryland Association of CPAs convention through July 5. Under the original schedule, I was to be walking into the convention on my last day, but I'm about thirty days behind schedule. So in the interim, I am walking in Maryland until I get back to Ohio next week.

We have completed about 2,200 miles.

When I was walking today, I ran into a friend of mine. He and I met through a mutual friend, Ed Arnold, years ago.

Ed built two very successful companies, and he and his wife, Jeannie, are major philanthropists in the United States. Their generosity is overwhelming.

Ed and Jeannie decided to sacrifice short-term pleasure for the long-term benefit they could provide to their employees and to society with their charitable giving.

I have been surprised so far of the challenges in the first 2,200 miles of the walk. But the long-term benefits are worth it for the short-term discomfort, because these children are so critically important to us.

We have two choices: either take the short-term pleasures but pay for it in the long run or accept short-term discomfort for a tremendous result in the long run.

Meaningful solutions require long-term thinking. So does our faith.

Life Lessons Learned: **Major problems require meaningful solutions geared to the long-run solution and not short-term appeasement.**

July 2, 2014

Tom Hood, Debbie, Donna, Pam and Andrew, and the entire staff of the MACPA were so kind as to allow Good Shepherd Services to have a fund-raiser at the beach retreat.

They surprised me in that Michele Wyman, the president of Good Shepherd Services, and Diana Ellis, our director of development, came to Ocean City to join with us in the awareness campaign.

I am at the site of where I will be walking into the Atlantic Ocean in mid to late August. The entire group was so supportive of our walk and our children.

We only have about 610 miles to go.

It came to me that this walk has been a spiritual uplifting because of the genuine goodness of so many people.

My wonderful niece Karin Lancelotta asked about us getting together, and I told her, "Karin that would be outstanding! I expect to get into Ocean City sometime after August 15 to August 20."

July 3, 2014

I hope everyone has a very happy and safe Fourth of July!

It's a great weekend to spend time with family and friends and just relax a little.

Today was great for walking as well as spending time in class with my friends at the Maryland Association of CPAs. Tom Hood and the entire MACPA team have been so supportive of our efforts at Good Shepherd. In addition to help promote the cause, Tom and the MACPA were so incredibly supportive of me when I deployed in the Marine Corps.

I remember so clearly on September 11, 2001, when our nation was attacked and I was eventually called to deploy to US Central Command, when the entire MACPA team helped me and my family despite the fact that I was leaving them high and dry relative to instructing for them later that year and early into 2002. They never complained. I am so grateful for their friendship.

We completed fifteen miles.

I am looking forward to getting back on my track in Ohio and resuming the walk outside of Springfield, Ohio, but at the same time, I am beginning to realize that the walk is coming to an end—a bittersweet time.

Today was my dad's birthday. I cannot begin to tell you how much I miss him and pray for him each day. I hope he is proud of what we are trying to do for our children.

July 4, 2014

It is our nation's birthday, and I am walking in Hurricane Arthur rains. The downpour was atrocious even though the day started out relatively calm. The calm ended pretty quickly, but then again, you can only get so wet! ☺

On Facebook, I asked,

> *Please use this day, our day of independence, to thank a veteran or service member for helping to keep us free.*
>
> *I am particularly thankful for our freedom of religion and freedom of assembly!*
>
> *It's why my walk is also a walk of gratitude.*

This year, like in years past, I had the chance to spend the holiday with my dear friend from the Archdiocese of Baltimore, Ashley Conley, and her husband and their family. Ashley is a devoted Catholic, mom, and spouse and, as importantly, dedicated to our Savior and his holy mother.

Her dad and her husband were both marines, so I feel as if I really am with family.

July 5, 2014

July 6, 2014

We are heading back to Ohio!

There were some good miles completed in Ocean City, and we did some hill trails today. Looking forward to hitting the mountains in West Virginia! ☺ Assuming of course that the mountains do not hit me first!

I love the change of scenery during this walk. I am trying to keep my ankle swelling under control for the final 570 miles of the journey. The swelling is continuing, and I hope that the damage to the ankle does not prevent me from finishing.

July 7, 2014

I told our spiritual chaplain,

> *Father Bill can't wait to see you. The strangest thing about the ankle is there's no discomfort at all. Just swelled up and I can't seem to get my shoes tied around the ankle. Think it has to do with the bone spur. Will get it checked out after I'm done this walk.*

Since I am still on the lecture circuit to help pay for the walk, we are walking in Park City, Utah, right now and get back to Ohio on Wednesday to continue my trek into Columbus, Ohio, by this Friday or Saturday morning.

I am looking forward to getting back on the trail for the walk, but I have to admit that hiking today at seven thousand feet was a blast. It was reminiscent of my walks across United States earlier during this walk in March and April.

July 8, 2014

The reaction in Park City, Utah, to the mission of taking care of our children has been overwhelming.

I saw the Miner's Hospital building in Park City, which dates back to 1904, and thought of how medicine has changed since then.

I am praying and have faith that in the hundred years when this walk is over, there will be someone looking back at all you have done to make a difference in the lives of so many children. It all starts with one child at a time.

We expect that we will be in Columbus, Ohio, by Saturday AM and then back on the trail.

July 9, 2014

A friend asked me if I planned on stopping by the Ohio Society of CPAs during my journey. I said,

> *Michael I plan on stopping in to the Ohio Society either late Friday or early Monday morning so I can see them to say hello. I have a support vehicle with me so it might mean I'll just backtrack to get into see them since I'm coming in on the weekend.*

July 10, 2014

We heard some very sad news while on the trail today. I would really love to have you pray for two dear friends and their families today. I just found out during my walk that two very close military friends have died: one today and one on July 5.

Lieut. Col. Bill Kane, Knight of Malta, passed away on July 5. Bill and I did the pilgrimage in Lourdes and became very close friends. Bill called himself my straight man for my jokes. He was a great American and will be truly missed.

Capt. Marshall Hanson, United States Navy reserve retired, passed away today. Marshall was an absolute patriot!

Both of my friends have passed over the bridge of eternal life to a life with our Savior and the Blessed Mother and all the same.

To Bill and Marshall, we are going to miss you. Until we meet again.

Semper Fi brothers!

July 11, 2014

The trend of having only met positive people is still continuing in Columbus and Ohio.

Today was exceptional, though, because I probably ran into fifty.

We did not get a lot of miles from the time I started this morning until evening because everybody was so supportive and wanted to hear about the mission, but then again, that is what the walk is about.

We did make it to the Ohio Society of CPAs, and as usual, the welcome was fantastic.

I am east of Columbus, on my way to Zanesville.

July 12, 2014

Today was too good to be true. I almost do not know what to say! I thought today's walk would be a quiet and reflective day.

A few days ago, when I stopped to check in the Super 8 in Reynoldsburg, Ohio, I met three wonderful people, well, actually four, because one of the young ladies was expecting. I started to pray for them.

Then today I met my long-term friend Shannon Bibbee and his wife, Amanda, and son Dylan. Their son Patrick was at home, and their daughter Paige is in heaven.

Shannon introduced me to wonderful people at lunch, such as Jeff and his wife, Michele. Jeff told me about relatives coping with developmental disabilities.

I was thinking about Paige and all the other wonderful children in heaven with our Savior and our Blessed Mother, when the solution for the problem of how to help children hit me like a bolt of lightning.

It is so incredibly simple, and I am stunned that I did not think of it before. I was so overwhelmed with emotion about the breakthrough that I just stopped on the side of the road and sobbed.

The Next Step—the Plan

The plan is very simple. We need to create a model to take care of children with emotional and behavioral problems and developmental disabilities independent of federal or state funding.

Within that mission and vision is the need to be good caretakers of the gifts that donors have provided us. Our strategy is simple yet complex.

We need to work closely with a university to develop a counseling model and treatment model based upon the faith of Saint Mary Euphrasia and the Sisters of the Good Shepherd.

We must work with Good Shepherd Services with this university and the sisters to provide feedback and continuous improvement to our treatment plans for the children.

We must develop a continuum of care to include the families and loved ones of our children.

We must break the cycle of trauma that affects so many of our children.

We must work with researchers to understand the causal factors influencing developmental disabilities.

It really is that simple. Many details are yet to emerge, but that it is the vision: create a model that breaks the cycle and continuously reinforces itself with the lessons learned as we help "one child at a time."

Paige, thank you for the inspiration for putting in a good word to the Holy Spirit for all of us.

Life Lessons Learned: **The best solutions are simple and inspired by God.**

Seeing Shannon, Amanda, Dylan, and so many new friends today gave me unbelievable energy to get some serious miles in.

We are almost to Zanesville, Ohio, and I am feeling like the weight of the world has been lifted from my shoulders due to the wonderful inspiration that came today while praying for Paige Bibbee. What an inspiration that little child of God is!

I am on cloud nine, and I am almost sad that this walk is going to be coming to an end.

In response to a wonderful note that I received from my neighbors, Don and Becki, I said, "Becki that is the most beautiful expression of spirituality I have ever read! Thank you for sending it."

Another veteran that I was teasing in an ice cream shop said to me, "It was very nice to meet you and imagine our surprise when we found out you paid our bill. That was so nice, thank you very much! Happy walking!"

We have so much to be grateful for.

July 13, 2014

> July 13, 2014 - Day #121 - Cambridge, OH - 2377
> miles down, 429 left to go! 85% of the walk completed!

I was walking through Zanesville, Ohio, this morning. On the way through town, I passed by a veterans memorial. I was touched by the enormity of the message when I realized that every helmet in the monument was for a soldier in the conflict. It was so very solemn and touching.

I attended Mass at Saint Nicholas Church in Zanesville and was impressed with our priest and his message.

We are ending the day a little early just east of Cambridge, Ohio, and not too far from Old Washington.

Once again, I have to go to work tomorrow for one day before I return to Ohio Monday night.

I will be giving a lecture with my son Matt for the PICPA in Pittsburgh. I am looking forward to seeing him.

If all works out well, I should be able to get into Wheeling, West Virginia, by Tuesday night.

Today in Cambridge, I was stunned by the generosity of John as he stopped on his way to work to give me Gatorade and water. But that is not where his generosity stopped. John also told me that he was a foster parent. He almost teared up when I told him what we were doing at Good Shepherd.

Once again, the Ohioans are living up to the reputation of the rest of the nation for being a generous, compassionate group. I am almost beginning to enjoy this walking stuff! ☺

Notice that I said *almost*! ☺

July 16, 2014

Today, I am lecturing in San Diego where the walk across America began on March 15.

I get back to eastern Ohio and West Virginia Saturday and expect to be in Wheeling by Sunday and Pennsylvania by Monday evening since I'm only in West Virginia for a short distance.

July 17, 2014

It is back to Ohio tomorrow night.

I heard from a voice out of the past today when Jan Jensen sent me a note on Facebook. Her message hit the spot and brought back memories.

> *Jan great hearing from you. I'm at Paradise point until tomorrow and then I head back to Ohio. I'm working on some leads for your son by the way. Do you realize you're one of the first people I met on my journey?*

July 19, 2014

We are back on the walking trail and met two incredible people. The first is Scott White, whom I met a year ago at a conference in Boulder, Colorado. When Scott heard about the walk, he was very kind to get me a book with a beautiful spiritual inscription. The book was about the nutritional needs of such a training effort for endurance. His kindness had a huge impact on my ability to sustain the energy for this walk. It was great to see Scott again and to finally meet his wife.

Next, I was staying at a hotel after I got in at 1:00 AM to the airport on the way back to Ohio. At the hotel in Frederick, Maryland, I met a customer service representative by the name of Adrijana. Not only was she extremely professional and courteous, but she was explaining her story about emigrating alone from her native Bosnia to the United States for greater opportunities.

Life Lessons Learned: **Do not be afraid to tackle the unknown. Be a pioneer!**

Her English was impeccable, and I had no idea she was not a native of the United States. She explained that she wanted to do well in a country that provided such opportunities. I commended her for her tremendous efforts and her maturity.

We now have less than 390 miles to go! I am starting to get into some real serious hills! ☺

Weather permitting, I expect to cross into Wheeling, West Virginia, tomorrow.

The Appalachian Mountains are not as high as the Rockies, but in many cases, they are just as steep, and in some cases, the mountains are steeper than in the Rockies.

I am looking forward to crossing over these mountains.

We spent some time today on the rail trails in the area as I am heading into my final segment of the walk.

July 20, 2014

We crossed into West Virginia, and I am looking forward to the same type of wonderful hospitality that I see from our chaplain, Father Bill Kuchinsky.

Father Bill's my hero! I first met Father Bill in Lourdes on a pilgrimage, and we have become great friends since. He and Father Drummond are spiritual guides and examples for all of us to emulate.

We crossed the Wheeling suspension bridge! What an unbelievable experience. As we continue our journey eastward, I continuously am amazed at the engineering brilliance of those who founded our nation. The Wheeling suspension bridge was the first of its kind in the New World. When you see the bridge move as vehicles and foot traffic move over with great ease and safety, you cannot help but wonder how they came up with this idea.

Seeing this magnificent bridge and the beautiful mountains around it leaves me in awe. I thank God for the opportunity to do this walk.

With all the beautiful scenery, something unbelievable just happened!

I had been walking up and down hills of 8 to 10 percent inclines and declines most of the day. On the way to get back to my support vehicle, I met two gentlemen at the top of the hill, coming into Wheeling, and explained to them about what we were doing with this walk.

Not more than five minutes later, a group of youngsters from Saint Ignatius High School in Cleveland stopped to talk with me about the mission. The two gentlemen at the top of the hill told them about the walk. We had talked on the side of a fairly steep hill by the way. And little did we know that one of the people in the group was from Wheeling Jesuit and was very good friends with me, good friend Michael Scheerer from the Order of Malta.

Oh, the hills! What a blast walking on these hills. I have been surprised to see how many ten-degree slopes I have seen. They have not been too bad yet.

Something happened today that has not happened on this entire journey so far. We crossed into three states.

My time in West Virginia was short-lived because I went through the Northern Panhandle. We had a great experience with everybody I met, and I met a ton of folks.

We are now in Pennsylvania, your Washington, Pennsylvania. Once again, everyone in West Virginia and Pennsylvania has been extraordinary. One more fantastic day on the road!

July 21, 2014

Today, I heard from my dear friend Randy, whom I met in Indiana. He told me of his health, and I told him, "Randy I will say additional special prayers for you for your cure. That meal at IHOP has a special meaning to me because I met you!"

The memories are never-ending!

Life Lessons Learned: **Life is about memories. Cherish your family and friends.**

The hills on today's trip and for the past three days have been exhilarating. I love getting to the top of a fairly steep hill and then seeing what I am going to discover at the top. I feel like I am on a treasure hunt. I am excited to see what I will find!

Life Lessons Learned: **Embrace challenges and overcome them. The victory is exhilarating.**

July 22, 2014

We are climbing the summit in Fayette County, Pennsylvania! I mean that literally!

> *Halfway up the hill and climbing. With your prayers we got to the top! What a view! If you ever question whether or not there is a God I encourage you to visit here.*

I saw a powerful reminder that future generations benefit from the work of others. I saw a historical marker. It noted that General Braddock's forces in the 1750s cleared the land that I was walking on, and they averaged well under ten miles per day.

***Life Lessons Learned*: We often lay the ground work for future generations. Be considerate of those coming after us.**

I am able to walk over twenty-five miles per day because of what Braddock and his soldiers did over two hundred years ago!

Just think what we can achieve if we turn our lives over to our Savior and do work in his name and for our children and grandchildren. Imagine how future children of Good Shepherd will benefit.

We met more incredible people today.

On my way up to the summit in Fayette County, I met Jamie when I was getting my haircut. What a great guy, and he was so helpful and donated the haircut to Good Shepherd.

Then I was having lunch and met folks near Fort Necessity—tasty sandwich with great new friends.

Then as I was walking past Fort Necessity, Judy stopped me and said that she had seen me in Brownsville the day before. I explained to her what I was doing. She was so supportive that she donated a meal tonight for the effort. I told Judy I will be making a donation in her name to Good Shepherd as well.

We continued hitting the hills and eventually ended up just over the border in Maryland. I was wiped out, plain and simple. I was very fortunate to see a church, and I had the chance to pray and thank our Blessed Mother for caring for me during this entire journey, as I know she cares for our children. I thanked her for interceding for me with her Son, our Savior.

When I got to the hotel, I met Lori, who cheered me up and kept me motivated to do some more miles tonight.

July 23, 2014

Today we reached the outskirts of Frostburg, Maryland. Love these hills! I really mean it.

I am enjoying the exercise of going up and down some of the steepest inclines we have seen on this trip. It is invigorating, to say the least.

I am fascinated that each part of the United States is so different, and at the same time, people in this country are uniformly good people. Please do not ever lose faith in people.

Perhaps one of the most important lessons I have learned on this journey is that people are genuinely good people. Look for the good in people and you will find it. Look for the bad in people and you will become jaundiced.

Life Lessons Learned: Have faith in your friends and your community. They are genuinely good people. Accentuate the positive for positive results.

July 24, 2014

> July 24, 2014 - Day #132 - Frostburg, MD - 2,546 miles down, 260 left to go! 90.75% of the walk completed!
> — with Frank Ryan.

July 26, 2014

What a wonderful trip today. We crossed over the last major obstacle in terms of mountains. From this point on, the mountains get much smaller until they level out past Frederick, Maryland.

Great people today, and the string of only meeting positive people continues!

July 28, 2014

For the first time in a long time, I had no cell phone coverage.

The C&O Canal was beautiful. I also took part of the Western Maryland railroad trail when I could not take the highway on Route 40 due to road restrictions.

We are back on Route 40 now on my way to Hagerstown, Maryland. We are getting close to the finish line. I think I can smell Ocean City from here.

July 29, 2014

We finally made it to Hagerstown, Maryland! Historic Route 40 is a site for all of you to see. So much of our nation's history can be found on this national road.

We are continuing to run into some really great folks along the way.

We are on the way to Frederick and then a visit to Good Shepherd before I head to Ocean City and the end of our journey.

July 31, 2014

My good friend Bob Gainer and I tried to get together today as I walked through Frederick. Unfortunately, we were not able to connect because he got called into a meeting. Getting the message from him and knowing how much he cared meant a great deal.

> *Bob I'm on West Patrick now*

> *Bob I'm passing Frederick middle school now*

> *Bob sorry I missed you as well. I actually detoured a little bit of West Patrick to run into you. I was surprised Frederick is closer to Hagerstown than I thought. To cross the bay bridge I have to take a car. They won't let me walk across it. I make up the distance on the other side of the bridge.*

This was probably the most perfect weather we have had for walking since the trip began.

The temperature was in the midseventies with a light breeze, and we were walking in the shade most of the day! We were getting shade from either the trees or the buildings.

I had dinner with my son Walt this evening since he lives in Maryland. I love my children so much. Walt is a wonderful son and a great patriot. I am so proud of him.

We still have had only positive experiences this entire trip! What a great feeling that is to know that so many people care about our kids.

August 1, 2014

We stopped by Good Shepherd Services on our walk across America to Ocean City! The reception that we received from the entire team was outstanding. I was so happy to see Jamie Costello from ABC News, who has been a dear friend to me and our children during this entire trip.

Jamie is one of those people who believe in accentuating the positive. With attitudes like his and from what we have seen in my walk across the United States, I know we can overcome the problems and obstacles we face.

Thank you, Jamie!

After I left Good Shepherd, I ran into a wonderful couple who shared their faith and asked many wonderful questions about our mission and our children. You can see that caring expression in their eyes for our kids. Meeting them capped a great day for me.

August 2, 2014

I sent a message to the wonderful couple who meant so much to me:

> *Jedediah I was honored to meet you and your wife yesterday.*
> *You're in my prayers today. I will be posting the pictures*
> *of you and your wife and others tomorrow morning. It's a*
> *beautiful picture of you and your wife. You can tell that*
> *you're blessed family,*

We had one of the best mileage days of the trip today. I believe it is all because of the motivation from having had the time to talk to some of our children and to see our great associates at Good Shepherd yesterday.

The real credit for the Good Shepherd mission belongs to the sisters, the children, and our staff. It is very important to me that I do this walk for the right reasons. One is to atone, and the other is to be grateful. The credit belongs only to our Savior and the mission.

The kids were so happy with knowing how much you care about them. I wish you could have seen their faces and the tears in their eyes from your compassion. They know that you love them. You made their day as well as mine.

We are coming close to going under one hundred miles left to go, and I have to go to Monterey, California, to teach for two days. I will continue walking while away and will complete the journey on August 9, God willing.

After I got off Route 144, the Old National Pike, I took Frederick Road to going to Good Shepherd. I also went on to South Rolling Road before I got to Good Shepherd.

I am going to see my sister Patty Lou tomorrow morning.

August 3, 2014

> August 3, 2014 - Day #142 - Annapolis, MD - 2,715 miles down, 91 left to go! 96.77% of the walk completed!

I am really riding an emotional high from seeing the children, the staff, and the Sisters at Good Shepherd Services on Friday. That was really the end of my journey in my mind. It is also the beginning of us working together to resolve the problem of how we can help our children the most.

The adrenaline is beginning to pump harder as I realize that we now have less than one hundred miles to go to get to Ocean City.

I was so happy to see my sister Pat, who has been an inspiration to me. She is someone for whom I am extremely grateful. I pray for her health every day.

On my way to Monterey, California, to teach and then finish the journey when I get back home.

August 4, 2014

I met a wonderful family coming back from a reunion in Baltimore where they celebrated the birthday of one of the relatives who was 102. They were so kind and compassionate.

I also met a very devoted mom who has a child with Down's syndrome, and she was celebrating the work of the Sisters of the Good Shepherd and our staff.

I cannot begin to thank you all enough for the wonderful memories as we are now under one week to go until we touch base in Ocean City.

August 5, 2014

Comment to my dear friend Laura LaBeau: "Laura I will be done on Saturday at noon. Getting really close! :-)"

We are getting close, and the expected time that I will enter the Atlantic Ocean is Saturday at noon. Gotten really positive responses from folks I met who heard about the mission the Good Shepherd, and tomorrow, August 6, is the 150th anniversary of opening the mission in Baltimore.

I am so incredibly proud of the Sisters of the Good Shepherd and the mission. Please join with me in a prayer of gratitude for these wonderful women who dedicated their lives to our Savior and children.

Today, Diana Ellis posted this on our site:

> *This week* Good Shepherd Services' *board chair, Frank Ryan, is completing the last leg of his Walk Across America from California to Maryland (2,806 miles!!!) to raise awareness of the continued need to provide personalized, God-inspired care for children who have the ongoing need for emotional, behavioral and psychological healing. Follow the rest of his journey at* Walk Across America. *Good luck, Frank!*

I met a lot of really wonderful people today who were so willing to listen about our need to care for children.

The scenery was beautiful, and as our walk is coming to an end this weekend, God willing, I'm going to miss so many wonderful folks that I met along the way.

August 6, 2014

We are coming down to the wire, and I am back on the Eastern Shore within fifty miles of completing the walk.

I met some exceptional people on the return flight from Monterey, California.

In addition to the great flight crew on Southwest Airlines, to include a good friend, Tony, the rest of the flight crew was exceptional. Thank you.

I also ran into two sorority members of the Deltas who were so helpful during my entire journey. Elizabeth and Michelle, you represent the Deltas well.

Tomorrow's walk gets me to within twenty-two miles of Ocean City and the end of the walk.

On this 150th anniversary of the opening of Good Shepherd in Baltimore, I ask you to keep all our children, our staff, and the sisters in your prayers.

August 7, 2014

We just entered Delaware. We will be in Delaware for the next day and a half until I reenter Maryland briefly at Ocean City to walk into the ocean.

We met a very wonderful family today and saw the TV broadcast from ABC about the walk. They stopped to make a contribution and to say thanks to the sisters.

I was also so honored today that my dear friend Karl Ahlrichs stopped by on the Eastern Shore to visit with me and offer support. Karl is one of those good guys. His caring compassion for people is unparalleled, and I am honored to call him my friend and to spend some part of my trip with him. Thank you, Karl.

Some well-wishers were asking me where I was since I know so many people in Maryland. This is my comment to Greg Whitby:

> *Greg I'm sorry I missed you as well. I've been spending most of my day on route 404 and now I'm on Rt 113 Dupont Blvd. i'm going to enter into the ocean at the hundred and third Street in Ocean City on Saturday at noon if you happen to be around.*

August 8, 2014

We are nearing the end! Just crossed back into Maryland for the final leg of the journey. We are down to thirteen miles to go.

Your prayers, thoughts, and well-wishes have been a welcome relief to this journey.

August 9, 2014

Well, you did it. Your prayers, compassion, and well-wishes got me from the Pacific Ocean to the Atlantic Ocean.

We walked into the water just before noon. The entire trip was met only by positive people.

I brought a statue of the Virgin Mary holding the infant Jesus that I carried with me into the water. Just as the Blessed Mother watched over me during my entire journey and prayed with me to her Son, I wanted this gift to her children to be a reminder to them that we too will watch over them and protect them for our Savior and our Blessed Mother.

To top off the wonderful day, I had the chance to go to Mass before walking into the ocean!

We met many wonderful families today.

In a very touching gesture, a young couple came up and told me that they were getting away for their first vacation since they had two of their children with disabilities. They told me that their children were their lives. Incidentally, their children are both in their twenties. What courage! What love!

We met a fellow marine retiree who spent twenty-four years with the marine band, the President's Own! What a great American!

We met a wonderful family as well. They were so kind to allow me to spend part of the day with them.

For all of you during this incredible journey, thank you so much for
the memories.

Comment to Joe Simmers:

> *Joe I am forever indebted to you and Allison. You both got
> me back on track and help this old marine remember how
> to walk this kind of distance. I can never thank you enough
> for all that you did.*

Comment from Don Hager:

Congratulations, Frank and Good Shepherd Services.

Father Bill your prayers made this journey a piece a cake. Consider this as a walk for your dad and how much he means to all of us.

Comment to Alberto Nunez: *"It all started with you!! Thank you so much. God bless you."*

Karl you are the perfect example of a great leader and most importantly a great friend.

Tina if you remember you're one of the first people I saw as I began my journey. You've been in my thoughts and prayers this entire trip. God bless you.

David thank you for the kind words. With the leadership like yours our nation is in great hands. I still remember our meeting in the restaurant in Albuquerque.

Don I can't wait to see you and Becki when I return. Your comments throughout this journey have made it easier for me to continue. You motivated me.

August 30, 2014

My son Matt and daughter-in-law Gosia just gave me a wonderful Father's Day gift and birthday gift for when I was away. Matt and I work together, and for that, I am honored. Matt and Gosia are my heroes.

Seeing the map and the coins from every state I walked through brought back very fond memories of all of you that I met along the way.

Thank you for the memories! Thank you for loving our children! God bless all of you, and thank you for coming on this journey of a lifetime with me!

ZEAL, MERCY, RECONCILIATION, INDIVIDUAL WORTH

As we began our journey across the United States of America, I reflected that it was a walk of atonement and gratitude.

On March 15, 2014, my plan was to ask every person that I have hurt to forgive me, every person that I have disappointed to pray for me, and every person that I helped to help another. I prayed to our Blessed Mother to intercede for me with her Son, our Savior, that I might always acknowledge with gratitude all of life's blessings.

But God had a different plan for me. The walk was still a walk of atonement and gratitude, but it was a prayer walk for our children for whom I am grateful. I have Diana Ellis to thank for that!

I originally told everyone that I was taking this walk by myself. I thought I was by myself, but then I realized that I was never alone. That is why throughout this route book, the term *we* was used.

You see, what I learned from this walk was that our Blessed Mother, our Savior, and the Holy Trinity were always with me. Our Savior and his mom, now my mom, made sure that I was cared for.

From what I have learned during this walk, it is apparent to me that it is our responsibility to care for all our children, especially those with emotional and behavioral problems and developmental disabilities.

I realize that the issue requires us all to give a little of ourselves to help one another as others helped me throughout my journey. I was not alone during my journey. My Savior and the Blessed Mother were with me each step of the day.

We must get to work!

If you think the task is daunting, I merely encourage you to look at what General Braddock's forces did over two hundred years ago that paved the way for the walk I just completed.

The progress we need to make in helping our children will be done one step at a time. My walk across the United States was over five million steps. With your help and prayers, we completed the walk.

We have many steps to take, but take one step at a time and our mission shall be completed and our children and their families cared for.

Walk with me.

Life Lessons Learned: **A journey begins with just one small step. Make a difference in someone's life. By doing so, your life will make a difference.**

APPENDIX

February 10, 2014

To Whom It May Concern,

For 150 years, the Good Shepherd Sisters have provided loving service in the Archdiocese of Baltimore. Through Good Shepherd Services, a Baltimore-based residential treatment and special education facility for adolescent girls and boys who come from throughout the state of Maryland, the Sisters and their associates have provided faithful care to those they serve. As Maryland's largest provider of residential mental health care for teens, Good Shepherd Services plays a vital role within our archdiocese in serving all children regardless of the severity of their problems.

In commemoration of the dedicated years of service of the Sisters, and with the purpose of raising awareness for the loving care and mental health needs of many teenagers through the country, the Chair of Good Shepherd's board, Frank Ryan, has committed to 'Walk Across America' beginning on March 15th, 2014 in San Diego, CA. I personally know Frank and am aware of his commitment to the mission of Good Shepherd Services and to this walk. His love and dedication for Good Shepherd Services are admirable.

This letter is a sign of my support for Frank's Walk Across America, and I've invited him to reach out to the Catholic dioceses and ministries along his route for assistance. Whether it is prayers, food or a place to sleep at night, I warmly invite others to help Frank complete the Walk Across America.

With sincere gratitude and prayerful best regards, I am

Faithfully in Christ,

+William E. Lori

Most Reverend William E. Lori
Archbishop of Baltimore

Sisters of the Good Shepherd
Province of Mid-North America
7654 Natural Bridge Road
St. Louis, MO 63121-4989
(314) 381-3400
(314) 381-7102 Fax

March 12, 2014

To Whom It May Concern,

The Sisters of the Good Shepherd, an international religious Congregation, has a network of community based social services to help meet the needs of children, youth and their families. We are founded on the principle that "one person is of more value than a world," and operate a variety of social service programs in communities across United States and Canada.

The Sisters of the Good Shepherd first came to the United States in 1842, opening the first House of the Good Shepherd in Louisville, Kentucky in 1843. In response to the needs of the rapidly growing frontier and the difficulties faced by many women and young girls in this new country, Good Shepherd ministries spread rapidly throughout the U.S. Within a few years the Good Shepherd had opened houses for women and girls in St. Louis, Baltimore, Philadelphia, Cincinnati and New York.

This year marks our 150th year of existence in Baltimore, Maryland. To celebrate this important milestone, Frank Ryan, the Board Chairman of Good Shepherd Services in Baltimore, is walking across America to raise national awareness to the needs of teenagers who suffer from serious mental health issues.

Frank's commitment to our Mission and to helping youth in need is extraordinary. I strongly support Frank's Walk Across America. I am united with our sisters and Mission partners in prayer for Frank's safety and for the success of this endeavor.

Thank you in advance for your assistance.

Sincerely,

Sr. Mary Catherine Massei, RGS
Sr. Mary Catherine Massei
Province Leader

AREA CODE 505 831-8100

March 12, 2014

William Buttarazzi
RCM&D
555 Fairmount Ave
Baltimore, MD 21286

Dear Mr. Buttarazzi,

This is in reply to your March 11 email about the walk that Frank Ryan is doing across our Country. I note that Archbishop Lori has endorsed this effort to bring awareness for the needs of teenagers suffering from emotional, behavioral and psychological issues, often times related to abuse.

I am sharing your email with our Knight of Columbus State Deputy Peter Quichocho. My hope is that the Knights of Columbus will provide Frank the rides he needs from his stopping/starting points to a place where he can rest, possibly providing him fellowship and meals. If you want to reach State Deputy Quichocho directly his phone number is 505-867-5524.

I note that Frank will start his walk on March 15 in San Diego, CA and will be walking through the Archdiocese of Santa Fe from April 9-19 with two days in Albuquerque, one day in Edgewood, one day in Stanley, two days in Las Vegas, one day in Santa Rosa and three days in Tucumcari.

My prayers are with Frank who is a Knight of Malta, a combat decorated Colonel in the Marines and who serves as the Chair of the Board of Good Shepherd Services of Maryland

Sincerely yours in the Risen Lord,

+ Michael J Sheehan

Most Rev. Michael J. Sheehan
Archbishop of Santa Fe

cc:
Very Rev. John Cannon, Chancellor/Moderator of the Curia, Archdiocese of Santa Fe
State Deputy Peter Quichocho, 7207 Milan Hills Rd SE, Rio Rancho, NM 87144

300

The Roman Catholic
Diocese of Phoenix

400 EAST MONROE, PHOENIX, ARIZONA 85004-2336 TELEPHONE (602) 257-0030
OFFICE OF THE BISHOP

March 12, 2014

Dear Pastors, Parochial Administrators and Parish Life Coordinators,

Mr. Frank Ryan, chairperson of the Board of Good Shepherd Services, which supports the work of the Good Shepherd Sisters in the Archdiocese of Baltimore has committed himself to "Walk Across America".

Mr. Ryan will be leaving San Diego on March 14th with the goal of reaching Ocean City, Maryland on June 6th. He will be walking through the Diocese of Phoenix from March 24th to the 28th, from Buckeye to the Scottsdale/Mesa area, before heading northeast to Payson.

Should you be contacted by Mr. Ryan or others representing him during his days in the Diocese of Phoenix, I want to inform you that I support this effort to raise funds that will provide assistance to the work of Good Shepherd Services and their Baltimore based residential treatment and special education facility for adolescent girls and boys.

Archbishop William E. Lori has asked that Mr. Ryan be supported by prayers, food and perhaps a place to sleep at night, as he travels through the Catholic dioceses along his route.

Sincerely yours in Christ,

Thomas J. Olmsted

+ Thomas J. Olmsted
Bishop of Phoenix

Encountering the Living Christ

301

Gear	**Weather Conditions**
backpack with water	all
granola	all
protein bars	all
rain gear	snow, ice and rain
portable potty	all
ski mask	cold, snow, rain, ice
goggles	all in case
spare glasses	all
Orange safety vest	all
GPS tracker	all
battery backup for cell phone	all
Motrin	

Lessons Learned:
1. Do all walks in 8 mile blocks with 1 hour breaks between each
2. Change socks after 16 miles

Lessons Learned 09/02/2013 to 09/05/2013

Purpose: The four day period from 09/02/2013 to 09/04/2013 was intended to replicate the "Walk". We did four 32 mile days to test endurance, gear, physiology, diet and the like.

Lessons Learned: The lessons learned were significant:

1. Very small issues like blisters can have a huge effect on the walk and care must be taken to:

    a. Change socks every 8 miles
    b. Take NuSkin to cover blisters that do occur
    c. Break in all shoes well before the walk
    d. Hiking boots are best – sneakers were a disaster and caused ALL the blisters

2. The diet is HUGE

    a. High protein diet gave me much more energy that I thought
    b. Carbs had little to no effect
    c. Electrolyte drinks were better than water although recommend taking a little of each
    d. Eating must be continuous – grazing to use Michelle's words
    e. I found that my times deteriorated when I did not eat as much protein.

3. Gear:

    a. I do not need to carry as much water as I thought. Recommend one gallon of water and one gallon of electrolyte mix.
    b. Multiple changes of socks are needed
    c. An extra head cover is needed (plus one that I am wearing)
    d. One extra pair of shoes in the backpack
    e. Insolated "sun" blanket is helpful

f. 6,000 calories of protein, granola and the like to eat (graze) is important to keep up energy.

g. Spandex shorts as an undergarment are critical – chaffing under the arms and legs is huge when I start sweating.

h. A walking stick is essential for going DOWN hills. Uphills were never a problem but downhills became a huge problem.

4. Logistics

a. I hate to do this but a support vehicle is going to be needed due to number of days that are taking place – there are too many variables which make staying walking for a 9-10 hour period very difficult at best.   Just too much gear to carry.

b. In more populated areas, a support vehicle is probably not needed but it is until we get east of the Rockies.

c. Bathrooms – hate to say this but sanitation is going to be key – with the food consumed there is no way around this – to include discussing it. ☺

Net Result: I feel that the results of the test were MUCH BETTER than expected. I feel that with the support and more training, we are on track for a March 15th launch.   Only caveat, I MUST do at least two hours of stretching per day until I depart – walking was not the issue – muscle tightness was.

Printed in the United States
By Bookmasters